What's WRONG with the RIGHT Side of History

Exposing the Roots of Progressive Pathology

LEE HARRIS

BOMBARDIER
BOOKS

Published by Bombardier Books
An Imprint of Post Hill Press
ISBN: 979-8-89565-297-8
ISBN (eBook): 979-8-89565-298-5

Post Hill Press
New York • Nashville
posthillpress.com

Published in the United States of America
1 2 3 4 5 6 7 8 9 10

For Andy Fuson, Ellen Vivet,
Adam Linnel, and Mau Quezada

Through thick and thin

CONTENTS

CHAPTER ONE

WHOSE SIDE OF HISTORY ARE YOU ON?

Late on the night of October 16, 1859, the abolitionist John Brown, along with twenty-one other men, approached by stealth the United States Armory and Arsenal located in the quiet Virginia village known as Harper's Ferry. Though his ill-fated "raid" would turn John Brown into a legend, he was already a notorious figure on America's antebellum landscape. Notorious, that is, to those who opposed the abolition of slavery, but celebrated among a small elite made up of New England transcendentalists. His cause had already been championed by Emerson, Thoreau, and their circle of friends, despite the fact that they were aware of Brown's role in the most violent episode of the whole dismal saga of "Bleeding Kansas." This had occurred some three years earlier, when John Brown, accompanied by some colleagues as well as his sons, went to the homes of several proslavery men, called them outside, and murdered them in cold blood, while their families looked in horror and pleaded for their lives. The Pottawatomie massacre, as the killings came to be known, enflamed anti-abolitionist sentiment across the nation. Yet John Brown remained a hero to the transcendentalists.

Four years later, when Brown seized the arsenal at Harper's Ferry, again with the help of his allies and his sons, he managed to hold out for a couple of days. Though one of his sons, Oliver, was killed, Brown himself was taken alive. The raid was one of the first major events to receive instant national coverage due to the most recent technological miracle: the telegraph. The ineptly planned and poorly executed attack horrified much of the nation, both North and South. But not the transcendentalists. It was greeted with enthusiastic approval by both Emerson and Thoreau. Later, it came to light that several members of the Boston elite, committed abolitionists themselves, had known in advance of Brown's plan and had even given him financial aid for his rash venture.

During his trial and up to his execution by hanging, John Brown behaved with a calm dignity that belied his reputation as a wild-eyed fanatic, earning the respect even of the governor of Virginia. Among his transcendentalist sympathizers, however, Brown was viewed as both hero and saint. His death on the scaffold was compared to Christ's death on the cross. When the news of his execution reached Boston, church bells were rung in mourning. During the Civil War that followed just over a year later, he became a folk hero to the Union Army, which often marched to the tune of "John Brown's Body."

Southerners had a quite different opinion of John Brown. It is true that his raid had been a colossal debacle, but it soon came to light what Brown had hoped to achieve. Captured documents indicated Brown was planning to set off an insurrection among the slave population in Virginia, which he assumed would swiftly spread across the other Southern states. Brown had already purchased hundreds of Sharps carbines and thousands of pikes. These and the immense cache of arms taken from the federal arsenal at Harper's Ferry were to be distributed to the thousands of liberated slaves that Brown expected to rally to his sacred cause. As it turned out, not a single slave joined him.

Yet for Emerson and his circle, it was the thought that counted. There were those in Boston's abolitionist circles who had long pinned their hopes of ridding the land of slavery precisely through a violent uprising of the slaves themselves, though other leading abolitionists, such as the sensible William Lloyd Garrison, were vehemently opposed to the use of violence. For Southerners, too, it is the thought that counted. They knew that Brown had been plotting to set off a servile insurrection, and they knew that many of the leading intellectuals in the North, such as Emerson and Thoreau, bitterly regretted that his plot had failed.

Looking back today on John Brown's famous raid, liberal historians admire his dedication to the cause of freeing the slaves, and laud him as one of the sparks that set off the Civil War and even praise him as a fore-runner of the civil rights movement. Yet they fail to ask the simple but obvious question: What would have become of our country if John Brown had succeeded in his grand project of engulfing the Southern states in a servile insurrection?

There were few in the South who did not know about the horrors of servile insurrection. Even though the most memorable slave uprising on American soil had occurred roughly three decades before, the very name Nat Turner was still enough to conjure up horrors in the minds of all Southerners, who recalled the short-lived uprising in Virginia that he had led. When it was over, fifty-one whites were dead. They had been bru-tally murdered simply because they were white. To prove this point, after massacring the family that owned Turner, and who may well have had it coming, Turner and his followers were about to leave the farm when they remembered that a baby had been left behind in a crib. Obviously, no one was worried that the baby would identify them. But the baby was white, and God had told Turner that all the whites must be exterminated, male or female, tottering ancient or sleeping babe. Had not Jehovah commanded King David to do the same with the Amalekites, according to the first book of Samuel? "Do not spare them; put to death men and women, children and infants, cattle and sheep, camels and donkeys." And was not Jehovah guiding Nat Turner? Had he not in fact put a spot across the sun to reveal to Turner the time at which he should begin the holy massacre?

The child was quickly hacked to pieces, and the men sought out more whites to axe to death. Ten children of one family were decapitated. But the mayhem was quickly put to an end. The neighboring slaves did not rally to the cause. Quite the opposite. They helped round up Turner and his followers. In the aftermath, the mindless slaughter of whites on the part of the blacks led to mindless slaughter of blacks on the part of the whites, and endless nightmares for decades to come.

What would have happened if John Brown had succeeding in instigating even a handful of uprisings like Nat Turner's? The image of marauding slaves hacking to death white women and children would have been spread across the land by the sensationalist newspapers of the day. News of each new atrocity would have been quickly wired by the new telegraph to every town and city in the nation. The cause of abolitionism would have been damaged irretrievably. So, this is what happens when the slaves are freed? In the following election of 1860, the recently created Republican Party, which was already closely identified with the abolitionist cause, would certainly have gone down to abject defeat, taking with it with any hope of emancipation for the slaves for the foreseeable future. The relations between white and black might well have been permanently poisoned by the memory of the great servile insurrection of 1860.

The war that came about in 1861, the American Civil War, would end up costing around seven hundred thousand lives by the time it ended in 1865, but it would later be seen as a conflict in which both sides had, for the most part, behaved with decency and honor. White soldiers from both the North and the South were eventually able to reconcile, although while the war raged, most intelligent observers, at home and abroad, believed that the Union had been irreparably shattered, never to be united again. The statues of Robert E. Lee that we are today removing from their sites were far from controversial at the time they were dedicated. The fact that the most famous leader of the Confederacy could be honored by the men who had fought bitterly against him was a miraculous testimony to the astonishing strength of the American Union. But a servile insurrection, either as a prelude to the war, or as an event unleashed by the war, would have made such a reconciliation impossible. Men can forgive those who have tried to kill them honorably in war, but not those who had instigated the massacre of their wives and children.

Looking back, we know there were no successful servile insurrections before or during the Civil War. For a variety of reasons, the slaves remained essentially sane while the white folks seemed intent on exterminating themselves in one bloody battle after another. Had the leading lights among the transcendentalists had their way, it could have been unimaginably worse—a race war that would have inevitably led to a brutal and indiscriminate suppression, in which whites of the both the North and South would have been united in the belief that the black man was too dangerous ever to be freed.

Yet oddly enough, none of the great minds of the New England transcendentalists ever seemed to consider the hell that would have been unleashed if their Christ-like hero had succeeded. This failure to recognize the enormous cost of their own convictions was the troubling heritage of America's first true progressives, those advanced-thinking New Englanders who went by the curious and rather pompous title of transcendentalists. They believed that their transcendentalist God was on their side. They also believed that they were on the right side of history, which may explain why the prospective massacre of those on its wrong side occasioned them not a single qualm. What else do those on the wrong side of history deserve?

Since the day of the New England's transcendentalists, part of the creed of American progressivism has been that they were marching on the right side of history. As a proud progressive, President Barack Obama, for example, never had any doubts about where he stood: "And we call upon others to join us on the right side of history—for while small gains can be won at the barrel of a gun, they will ultimately be turned back if enough voices support the freedom of nations and peoples to make their own decisions." But President Obama also had no doubts who stood on the other side of history. In his first inaugural address, he asserted, "To those who cling to power through corruption and deceit and the silencing of dissent, know that you are on the wrong side of history." During his administration, he condemned Russian President Vladimir Putin and Syrian President Bashar al-Assad, among others, for being on the wrong side of history, leading conservative commentator Jonah Goldberg to write that the Obama administration "has used the 'the wrong side of history' phrase more than any I can remember," especially in regard to its foreign policy failures, after which Obama "or his spokespeople have wagged their fingers from the right side of history."

In an article in *Slate* magazine on April 17, 2014, Ben Yagoda notes "the dramatic rise in use" of wrong side/right side rhetoric "from the 1970s to the present," adding, with commendable understatement, that he didn't "have a sense that this was a period when people had developed a particularly penetrating understanding of history's arc. If anything, the opposite." Yagoda, however, notes that Democrats had no monopoly on such rhetoric. In the confirmation hearings for Chuck Hagel as secretary of defense, Senator John McCain castigated Hagel for his opposition, as senator, to the Iraqi "surge" by concluding: "History has already made the judgment about the surge, sir, and you're on the wrong side of it."

Since 2014, there has been an explosion of such rhetoric. It has become virtually ubiquitous, both on the Right as well as the Left. In 2019, conservative commentator and Obama critic Ben Shapiro boldly took up the phrase, so often associated with the progressive agenda, and used it in the title of a bestselling book: *The Right Side of History: How Reason and Moral Purpose Made the West Great*. The gist of his argument is that progressives like Obama were on the wrong side of history, while right-thinking conservatives like himself were on the right side.

The subtitle of Shapiro's book was important, in order to distinguish it from a quite different book called *The Right Side of History: 100 Years of LGBTQI Activism*. Indeed, the Human Rights Campaign, devoted to promoting the LGBTQ+ cause, sells for a modest $4.99 a wall poster to hang in your own home that reads simply: I STAND ON THE RIGHT SIDE OF HISTORY. But let us consider some other examples, drawn from a wide of array of individuals, many of whom might well be puzzled to find themselves on the same side of history.

On March 7, 2023, the *New Yorker* magazine published an essay by Emma Green entitled "The Right Side of History: How should historians respond to the urgency of this current political moment?"

Liberal Democratic Senator Chris Murphy has been quoted as saying: "I wake up ready to fight, and I feel like I am on the right side of history every day."

Shane Claiborne, an evangelical Christian leader and author, has said: "I would love to see the Church on the right side of history."

Actor Justin Bartha, star of the *Hangover* trilogy, said, referring no doubt to a different role: "It's not often as an actor you get to be involved with a project that seems to be on the right side of history."

Jerry Hawkins, the executive director of Dallas Truth, Racial Healing & Transformation, writes: "We need to understand our history and make sure we are on the right side of it."

António Guterres, general secretary of the United Nations, has proclaimed: "To all those working, marching, and championing real climate action, I want you to know that you are on the right side of history, and I am with you."

Chess grandmaster Garry Kasparov writes: "Values-oriented foreign policy of the free world would be much better supported by the self-awareness of being on the right side of history."

American football player Davante Adams put matter succinctly when he said: "It's good to be on the right side of history."

And who can doubt what a wonderful thing it must be to be on history's good side, and not its bad?

The brutal attack on Israeli civilians by the terrorist group Hamas on October 7, 2023, may have seemed to most civilized men and women like a reversion to barbarism that should have long since been relegated to the trash bin of history. Yet student protesters on many American college campuses, demanding a Free Palestine "from the river to the sea," quickly rallied around the slogan "We are on the right side of history." Needless to say, various radical student groups, like the SDS chapter at Florida State University, denounced their own universities for standing "with Zionism *on the wrong side of history* by perpetuating the epidemic of political repression spreading across the nation." [Emphasis added.] Other radical student groups might vary the rhetoric, but the theme was always the same: "We are on the right side of history, and those who oppose us are on the wrong side." Such student activists may even decorate the walls of their dormitories with a poster provided by the Palestine Poster Project Archives that exhorts, "Be on the Right Side of History!"

Beyond the campuses, many others supported their cause. On April 24, 2024, the radical socialist magazine *Jacobin* published an article by Ben Burgis entitled "Pro-Palestine Protesters Are on the Right Side of History." Only a month later, Iran's supreme leader Ayatollah Ali Khamenei wrote a letter to those American students, who by fervently chanting the slogan "From the river to the sea / Palestine will be free," had shown themselves to be "on the right side of history."

Clearly, those who claim to be on the right side of history make for strange bedfellows. The Human Rights Campaign is there, but so too is the Ayatollah Ali Khamenei, leader of one of the world's most homophobic regimes, Iran. Greta Thunberg stands next to Garry Kasparov, and while Ben Shapiro and Barack Obama may cast uneasy glances at each other, they too are somehow on the right side of history. But can everyone be on the right side of history? Obviously not. Either some people are seriously deceiving themselves, or there is something very fishy about the whole notion that history has a right side and a wrong side—something that, given both the omnipresence of this trope in contemporary discourse and the blatantly contradictory way in which it is currently thrown around, cries out for thoughtful examination.

The "right side of history" is, of course, a metaphor. Unlike a bed or a roadway, which have both a right side and a left side, no one has ever talked about being on the left side of history, especially not those on the Left. The true opposite of the right side of history has already become self-evident: it is the *wrong* side of history. But what sense can it make to speak of a right and wrong side of history unless history itself is inevitably marching toward a certain goal? Those who march with it are clearly on the right side of history, and those who try to impede this march are just as clearly on the wrong side. Even those who are not marching in step may fall into this category. Indeed, from the nineteenth century on, the belief that there was a right side to history was in fact predicated on the belief in an end of history. Karl Marx, for example, argued that with the achievement of true communism, after a long period of socialist development, secular history as we know it would simply come to an end. Hence, to be on the right side of history required both knowing (a) what the end of history would be, and (b) devoting yourself to achieving it through political action, if not revolutionary upheaval. In the early 1990s, however, this Marxist theme was given a whole new lease on life as a result of one of history's most shocking events: the failure of the first great experiment in practical Marxism known as the Union of Soviet Socialist Republics.

As we look back at the sudden and totally unexpected collapse of the Soviet Union that began in 1989, many of us may find it a challenge to remember the sense of historical optimism that filled the air at the time. The long and frightening Cold War that had commenced so quickly after the end of the Second World War was at last over. The Berlin Wall had fallen. The citizens of those captive nations newly liberated from the Soviet yoke, such as Poland and Czechoslovakia, filled their streets and squares with jubilant throngs. The wicked witch of the Soviet regime lay dead, and its former victims were overjoyed. The great rivalry between the USSR and the USA was finally at an end, a rivalry that many feared would lead one day to the nightmare of thermonuclear war and the end of civilized life as we know it. Surely, here was the dawn of a new world, one that would be free from all the evils and misery that had afflicted the twentieth century, with its bloody revolutions and horrendous world wars.

The future that had been envisioned by the Nazi regime, aka the Thousand Year Reich, had proved to be a lethal illusion, both for Germany and much of the rest of the world, while the future that had been envisioned by the Soviet commissars had suddenly collapsed beneath their feet. There was now, so it seemed, only one vision of the future left standing. And, luckily, it was our own—the vision of liberal democracies inevitably sprouting up around the globe. Instead of seeing this outcome as the result of a fortuitous concatenation of unforeseeable circumstances, a new historical paradigm emerged. Our victory had been inevitable. All history had been moving toward this moment of triumph.

This mood of optimism helps to explain the immense enthusiasm that greeted the publication of the book *The End of History and the Last Man* by American political scientist Francis Fukuyama. Appearing as it did in 1992, shortly after the collapse of the USSR, Fukuyama argued that the dream of a socialist future had finally been exploded and that there would be no longer be any great ideological rivalry among the nations. Henceforth all would embrace the one remaining option and become like us in the USA or our cousins in the advanced nations of Western Europe, liberal capitalist democracies.

Like all thoughtful books that end up bestsellers, *The End of History* had two separate lives. First, there was the nuanced argument put forth by the scholarly Fukuyama. He certainly did not expect history to end in the normal sense of the word. There would be new elections, new presidents, even new governments. There could be all sorts of crises caused by natural disasters. There could even be wars. Furthermore, his thesis had nothing triumphalist about it. On the contrary, one gets a sense of regret on Fukuyama's part that the virtues honored by previous ages, especially the aristocratic ones, such as heroism, had become relics of the past.

Second, there was the book that was reduced to the slogan "the End of History." In this simplified distortion of the thesis, the United States and its allies had triumphed over the forces of evil and were now in a position to dictate a "new world order," as President George H. W. Bush phrased it. Meanwhile, the liberal media found a host of different color-coordinated revolutions in nations that lacked any tradition of self-government but that were sure to be thriving liberal democracies within a few weeks. A tidal wave of such revolutions seemed on the verge of ushering in a new Islamic Golden Age, yet not even one lof these hopeful revolutions came close to fulfilling the heady expectations the Western media had set for them.

Nonetheless, Fukuyama's basic thesis, qualify it as much as you wish, is still a modern variant of the Marxist notion that history was moving to an inevitable end and that once this point had been reached, there could be no further need of that messy thing called history. Karl Marx had been right, after all, that there would be an end of history, only he had bet on the wrong horse. It was capitalism and not socialism that had made it across the finish line, democracy and not the dictatorship of the proletariat. Yet only a little more than a decade after the demise of the Soviet Union, there came another bolt out of the blue, this time quite literally when two airplanes flown by Islamic terrorists rammed into the Twin Towers on September 11, 2001.

With the fall of the Twin Towers, the optimists of the West became painfully aware that there were those who fanatically hated our idea of the future and who wanted no part of it. The followers of radical Islam entertained a very different notion of the end of history. They had no doubt that it would come, and they knew precisely the shape it would have. It would be a world in which all human beings had become what Allah had intended them to be all along: devout Muslims. The "House of Peace" (*Dar al-Islam*), would then extend across the entirety of the globe. That was their future, and it was obviously inconsistent with our own ideas of our future. At the heart of this conflict was not the clash of civilizations but the clash of two radically different visions of humanity's future.

But rather than abandon its pet future, the United States and its allies decided to double down. If some in the Middle East were reluctant, or even hostile, to our vision of the future, we would use our immense military superiority in order to remove and defeat them. What followed was the attempt to clone Western liberal democracy in the Arab world, starting with the toppling of Saddam Hussein's regime in Iraq. One of the best-selling books of that time, *The Pentagon's New Map: War and Peace in the Twenty-First Century* by Thomas P. M. Barnett, argued that once this had been achieved, there would be a spontaneous revolution through the Muslim world, with the people demanding the same kind of blessings that they saw overflowing in the newly remodeled Iraq. Meanwhile, neoconservative David Frum, who unlike other neocons was not content with merely seeing the end of history, coauthored a book that went one step further, foretelling *An End to Evil*.

There were to be further surprises. Though the USSR had been broken into various smaller nations, by far the largest piece, old Mother Russia, still remained. According to the end-of-history scenario, Russia, having broken the ideological fetters of Soviet Communism, would naturally turn into the same kind of liberal capitalist democracy that we in the West enjoyed. Instead, post-Soviet Russia rapidly plunged into an economic tailspin. The old assets of the USSR, those ill-run factories producing inferior products, and even then, not nearly enough of them, became the spoils of the ill-famed oligarchs, whose ruthless greed made the Mafia look like a ladies' reading club.

It had always been assumed that the transition from capitalism to socialism was the final stage of history. Socialism's many critics had always warned that it would fail, but no one had given any thought to what would happen *after* it failed. Indeed, only fringe elements, like Ronald Reagan and a few other crackpots, even imagined that the Soviet Union could collapse in the first place. Hence, there were no experts who had given any thought to how a Communist regime, in which the capital assets were all owned by the state, could redistribute those assets in a fair and equitable way back to the people. If they had given it any thought, they would have quickly realized that in slicing up such a gigantic pie, those with the dirtiest fingers would come away with the biggest pieces. And they did.

A decade later, former KGB agent Vladmir Putin began his ascent to supreme authority in the New Russia, and with him came a resumption of Old Russia's claim to be a Great Power on the world stage. This was certainly not the role that the triumphant Western democracies had assigned to it in their new world order. Russia was supposed to assume the far humbler role of a mere regional power, to quote President Barack Obama. Such presumption on Russia's part seemed folly to many in the West, considering its declining birthrate and soaring levels of alcoholism, and the fact that its economy was more suitable to a small Balkan nation than the vast Russian expanse.

Putin's Russia, however, presented something genuinely new under the sun. Of old, if a nation wished to remain a formidable military power, it had to remain a strong economic power as well, and this became even more essential as technology played an increasingly decisive role in warfare. It took a great army to hope to survive against another great army, and the soldiers had to be equipped with weapons at least as good (and hopefully better) than their enemies. Therefore, when a nation underwent a drastic economic decline, it lost its standing as a power to be reckoned with. This logic, however, did not apply to nuclear weapons. A nation that amassed a large arsenal of such devices could be reduced to economic subsistence and yet remain a formidable threat so long as it was able merely to maintain its arsenal in good working order. Indeed, if we look at North Korea, we will find a nation where many of its people are actually on the verge of starvation, living in an economic wasteland, yet whose leaders have realized that even a small nuclear arsenal gives them enough clout to keep the world on edge. Yet their arsenal pales in comparison to that of Russia, where there are more than enough nuclear warheads to carpet-bomb the planet back into the Stone Age.

Meanwhile, back in the West, the neoconservatives, alarmed by the threat posed by Russian expansion, decided that the best policy would be to bolster the defenses of those nations neighboring Russia that were once republics of the USSR, like Ukraine and Georgia, or its satellites, such as Poland and Romania. Forgotten was the promise that the Western leaders of the time had made to the last Soviet premier, Mikhail Gorbachev, that they would not take advantage of the Soviet Union's decline and dismemberment in order to advance their own interests. Instead, there was a steady expansion of Western power into Eastern Europe, a process whereby the former satellites and even former republics of the old USSR became members in good standing of their old adversary, the North Atlantic Treaty Organization (NATO).

It has now become a commonplace to refer to the *New* Cold War. There has even been a bit of nuclear saber-rattling from Russia, while China is threatening to become the next economic superpower, proving that liberal democracy is not the only path to worldly riches. Thus, within three decades, the dream of the end of history had revealed itself to be a mirage. But then history has never been kind to any of the earlier triumphalist visions of its demise.

By 221 BC, the first emperor of China, Qin Shi Huang, had successfully united the various warring factions that had plagued China for centuries. One of his first acts was to command that all previous books and records of the Chinese be gathered together and set ablaze in what may have been the largest bonfire in human history. In doing so, the mighty emperor believed that by abolishing the past, he had brought history to an end. There were to be no more divisions, conflicts, or wars in the Celestial Kingdom. Qin Shi Huang, however, was not so sure that the afterlife would be equally peaceful, which might explain the immense Terracotta Army of eight thousand soldiers he commanded to be buried with him. Or perhaps he planned to bring the same peace and order to heaven that he had established on earth. The revenge of history, however, came swiftly for the Qin Dynasty, which, despite its boasts of immortality, lasted a mere fifteen years, although two years longer than The Thousand Year Reich imagined by the Nazis.

With the failure of the most recent end of history, we find ourselves back at the drawing board, where we must confront those big questions that are the domain of the philosophers of history. Does history have a meaning? Is it irresistibly moving toward a certain goal, and if so, what is it? Can we know this goal in advance and consciously work toward it ourselves? Is history a steady progress upward and onward, or is it just one damn thing after another, without rhyme or reason? In this course of this book, we will examine how various thinkers of the past have grappled with these questions, from the time of ancient Greece to our current world. As we will see, the idea that history has a right side and a wrong side arose very late in the annals of ideas. No one before the nineteenth century saw history in this light.

Above all, it is necessary to confront the myth of the right side of history, not merely to gain greater philosophical clarity, but because it is a dangerous myth that in the past has been used to justify the dehumanization, brutalization, and murder of millions of people for the sole crime on being judged to be on the wrong side of history. Indeed, those most supremely certain they are on the right side of history are most likely to stop at nothing to achieve their goal, as the New England transcendentalists clearly demonstrated by hero-worshiping the zealot John Brown, whose dream of drenching the hated South with blood they fully shared.

Today, we are confronted with zealots who are equally sincere in their belief that they are on the right side of history. They call themselves "woke," an indication that they alone are wide awake in a world full of sleeping sheep. They see themselves as the advance guard of humanity, leading the way to their brave new world. They champion a variety of causes that on the surface appear to have absolutely nothing in common: open borders, transgender rights in competitive sports, radical climate activism, gender education for five-year-olds, packing the Supreme Court, eliminating Israel, and a host of others that go to make up what has been dubbed the "Omnicause." Those seeking an ideology behind this strange smorgasbord of causes—cultural Marxism or postmodernism, for example—certainly have their work cut out to find a central theme. It is a bit like trying to find resemblances among the various freaks at an old-fashioned carnival sideshow: the geek, the fat lady, the bearded lady, the dog-faced boy, the sword-swallower, the dwarf, the strongman. Their only commonalty was their freakishness, their deviation from the norm. This too is at bottom what the woke all have in common: not a coherent ideology, just their smug and haughty rejection of the ideas and values of Middle America. And, of course, their fanatical conviction that they alone are on the right side of history and that others are not marching nearly fast enough.

No one is quite sure who first coined the phrase "the right side of history," though it is generally agreed that it originated during the nineteenth century. This was no accident. It was this century, after all, in which the idea of progress first began to stir men's souls. It was part of the zeitgeist. By the nineteenth century, the erosion of the Judeo-Christian tradition that had begun during the Enlightenment reached its climax. French philosophers, like Voltaire, had tirelessly mocked the old idea of Divine

Providence, with its comforting assurance that whatever happened, it had to be for the best. But what could possibly take its place? The answer offered by the nineteenth-century visionaries was faith in the Future.

Notice the capital *F*. It is significant. For the nineteenth-century visionaries were not interested in our everyday notion of the future with a small case *f*, the prosaic future that awaits every morning and of which we make the best we can. Their idea of the Future was blazed in neon lights. It was no longer your future, or mine, or our neighbors'. It was the Future of all mankind. And it was coming—of that the visionaries had no doubt. For the many who had lost their faith in God, this Future became an ersatz religion, designed to offer the comfort and hope that Christianity had once provided. Faith in God was replaced by faith in the Future. The various sects of those new faiths had their own names—Fourierism, Marxism, Owenism, transcendentalism, social Darwinism, fascism, and anarchism, among others—but all worshipped at the Temple of the Future.

The historical optimism introduced by the Future Revolution of the nineteenth century had no precedent. It was certainly not shared by the ancient Greeks, and indeed it would have been incomprehensible to them. They were convinced that mankind's best days had already passed and that what awaited the race of mortals was only an increasingly bleak future. This pessimistic view received its classic expression in the Greek poet Hesiod, who lived sometime in the sixth century BC. In his poem *Work and Days*, he lists a series of epochs: the Golden Age, the Silver Age, the Bronze Age, the Heroic Age, and the Iron Age.

In the Golden Age, men did not need to labor to produce their daily bread. The earth was so bountiful with its fruits that there was no need to plant or to plow the fields, in fact, no need of agriculture at all. The Silver Age, while still rather pleasant, represented a decline, as did the Bronze and Iron Ages, with the Heroic Age, as might be expected, being an exception to the rule of general decay. Yet, for Hesiod, as for the Greeks in general, the maxim was, Things were bound to get worse over time, along with a general increase of human toil and misery.

Hesiod was a poet who lived before philosophy emerged in Greece, but later thinkers, such as Plato, were in agreement with his basic thesis that the world was bound, over the long run, to get worse and worse. As historian of ancient Greece J. B. Bury observed in his book *The Idea of Progress*, "If some relative progress might be admitted, the general view of Greek philosophers was that they were living in a period of inevitable degeneration and decay—inevitable because it was prescribed by the nature of the universe." Plato, for example, argued in *Timaeus* that the deity, whom he called a "demiurge," had created the universe as perfect as he could, but that it would deteriorate over time. The universe, Plato believed, would last 72,000 solar years. The first 36,000 years had held up rather well. It was here that Plato located the Golden Age, but we were now living in the second 36,000-year period, when we could only expect to see an ever-increasing descent toward universal senescence. Yet, for Plato, that was not the end of the story. For a new universe would come into being, and it would go through the same cycle all over again. The Hindu worldview also held that the universe went through cycles of decay and rebirth, though each cycle was immensely, mind-boggling larger than the mere 72,000 years Plato had envisioned.

Those Romans who turned their attention to such deep questions echoed Greek pessimism. Lucretius, both poet and philosopher, was aware that mankind had indeed made progress from its original bestial state. Fire had been mastered, followed by invention of language, the development of arts, the creation of crafts and industries, along with the increased improvement in social organizations by customs and laws. Yet, strange as it appears to us, Lucretius believed that all such progress was over and done with by the time he himself arrived on the scene. The age of invention and improvement lay in the past, not in the future. The idea that progress had already reached its limits would have a long life, and it has been revived in our own day in the anti-technological movements that we will examine later in this book.

The more thoughtful of the ancients, dismissive of the vulgar superstitions of the people, had a more philosophic attitude toward the future.

Though they naturally had a variety of views on the topic, there was a basic consensus: the future was not in the hands of the gods but was the product of an impersonal and inexorable power, which we call Fate, the Latins called Fortunata, and the Greeks Tyche. Whatever name it went by, it was utterly beyond our control. There was no pattern to history, and certainly no right and wrong sides to it. Classical fatalism precluded all such ideas.

Before the ancient Greeks invented the study of history, there were obviously all sorts of events going on in the world of both great and small consequence. Yet there was no history. The order of the world was marked by the seasons. Each year was simply a repetition of the year before, as the next year would be a carbon copy of its predecessor, with minor variations. Every now and then there would be catastrophe: forest fires spread across the land, volcanoes erupted, and earthquakes shook down hovels. At other times, catastrophe would come at the hands of man, as predators suddenly appeared in the midst of a peaceful village to steal the inhabitants' scanty stores of grain. Things happened, but nothing was recorded. This was the general condition of the human race. The eternal present was the rule. Surprises were simply freaks of nature.

Yet in even the most primitive tribes, an event or an individual would stand out that was worth talking about. Sometimes people would remember them and pass on oral accounts. A mighty king ruling over a vast empire might carve his victories and achievements on monuments designed to perpetuate his name through all the ages to come. But until the Greek historians appeared, no one ever thought of history as a special field of inquiry, requiring certain methods, and whose aim was to provide a reasonably objective portrayal of both characters and events. More impor-tantly, no one thought of history as a story—a tale with a beginning, a mid-dle, and an end, pointing out moral lessons both for individuals and for the communities of which they were a part. Yet there is one theme that prevails in the writings of all the ancient Greek historians, namely that it was both foolish and dangerous for men to believe that they could control their own fate or shape history as they wished. This fatalism is so contrary to the idea of progress that the modern age takes for granted that we should pause a moment to consider what lay at the heart of this bleak assessment of man's capacity to direct his own destiny.

The ancient Greeks had a word to express the heady overconfidence that can lead men, both as individuals and as whole communities, to their ruin. This state of mind they called *hubris*, and it is a topic to which the Greeks continually return, both in their tragedies and in their histories. *Hubris* is often translated into English as something like "overweening pride," but the catastrophe that overtakes *hubris* is not brought about by pride alone, no matter how excessive. Rather, it is the result of the proud man's deluded conviction that he can control his own destiny and that his plans for the future cannot possibly fail. The law of unintended consequences may foil lesser mortals, but not him.

The first history ever written, Herodotus's *The Persian Wars*, is full of cautionary tales about the folly of hubris. Perhaps the most famous is the story of Croesus, whose name has been preserved for us in the phrase by which we often designate a fabulously wealthy man when we say, "He is as rich as Croesus." Reputed by his contemporaries to be not merely rich, but at the very top of the *Forbes* list of the Richest Men of the Ancient World, Croesus was also obnoxiously insistent that he was the happiest man as well.

Croesus was particularly insistent on this point when he was visited by the Athenian legislator Solon, renowned for his wisdom. Exhibiting his heaps of treasure to his honored guest, Croesus eagerly asked if this vast wealth did not prove him to be happier than any other mortal then alive, to which Solon replied with the words: "Count no man happy until he dies," which was his way of saying, "You may be happy today, but who knows what the future holds?" But Croesus was unimpressed and took no notice of Solon's ominous hint. For Croesus believed that, in addition to be very rich, he was also very lucky, supremely confident that any future venture he undertook was bound to be a success. Having already conquered many of the neighboring kingdoms and rendering them tributaries to Lydia, he was sure that his next conquest, that of Persia under the rule of its parvenu king, would also turn out in his favor. Yet in order to obtain complete certainty about his future prospects, he dutifully sent to the oracle of Delphi to discover what she had to say about the matter. He was delighted to hear her verdict. She completely agreed with him: if he invaded Persia, she assured him, a mighty empire would fall.

And it did. Only it was the kingdom of Lydia, not that of Persia. When taken prisoner by the Persian king, who turned out to be Cyrus the Great, the bitterly disappointed Croesus finally saw the error of his ways, his blind faith in his own luck and his foolish delusion of being the happiest man on earth. This was certainly not how Croesus felt as he awaited execution at the top of the huge funeral pyre that had been erected to send him off into another world. Herodotus tells us that Croesus cried out, expecting them to be his last words: "Solon! Solon!" Upon hearing this, Cyrus had the incipient flames doused and asked Croesus what he meant by these mysterious words. This gave the forlorn king the opportunity to tell Cyrus about the wise counsel that had been offered to him by the Athenian sage, but which he had so foolishly ignored. Cyrus was impressed and Croesus was saved.

Leading him down from the pyre, Cyrus took his former enemy and made him one of his most intimate confidants, whose advice he would continue to consult for years and which, according to the account of Herodotus, invariably proved to be both prudent and sober. Perhaps Cyrus was himself saved from future acts of hubristic folly by heeding the warning of the man who had known the most extreme reversal of fate, recognizing a truth that is too often overlooked, namely that the man who has known bitter failure is not infrequently a better counselor than the man who has known only success.

Such pessimistic assessment of man's capacity to shape his own destiny presents the sharpest challenge to those who believe they are on the right side of history, or who are convinced that by their own political actions they can be preparing for the end of history. To the Greek mind, it was all vain delusion and arrogance. And yet, with only a few lonely exceptions, in the modern world, thinkers both on the Right and Left of the political spectrum reject this pessimism, fully convinced that they possess roadmaps to guide us to a better world in a better future. How such an optimistic view of history emerged out of the pessimism of the classical world will be examined in the following chapters.

CHAPTER TWO

THE SEARCH FOR PATTERNS IN HISTORY

Few of Martin Luther King's many memorable phrases have resonated as much as those he spoke on March 31, 1968, at the Washington National Cathedral when he said that "the arc of the moral universe is long, but it bends toward justice." Here was something radically different from the pessimism of the classical world. The universe was not tending to degeneration and decline. It was not indifferent to us. It had a moral dimension and, more astonishingly still, it was bending toward justice, and not increased wickedness. Rather than getting worse and worse, the moral universe was getting better and better. Such optimism would have shocked the classical mind. Yet King's words were quoted and celebrated as if they were self-evident truths. Something had definitely changed since the time of the ancient Greeks and Romans. This something was Christianity, whose advent demanded the rejection of classical fatalism in all its forms. History ultimately made sense, because it was in the hands of a loving God.

Dr. King was a Baptist minister, and in his famous quote about the arc of the moral universe, he may well have merely been expressing a sentiment common to Christians since the first century AD. History was in the hands of God, a wise and loving God, who despite the trials and tribulations suffered on earth by his own faithful people, would nevertheless make things right in the end, when God's justice would at last prevail.

The idea of Divine Providence has an ancient lineage, adumbrated in the Hebrew Bible but given its classic Christian formulation by Saint Augustine of Hippo in his book *The City of God*, which first appeared in 425 AD. In this massive work, Augustine writes "that God can never be believed to have left the kingdoms of men, their dominations and servitudes, outside of the laws of His providence." Providence governed all things, a tenet accepted by every Christian sect in the following centuries and which remains an article of faith to many Christians today, though even the most devout among them take out insurance policies on their homes. As late as the nineteenth century, however, such commonsense prudence was seen by some as blasphemous. Henrik Ibsen, in his play *Ghosts*, offers us a character who is firmly opposed on religious grounds to the very idea of insurance. He is Pastor Manders, whose close friend, the wealthy widow Helen Alving, has provided the funds to build an orphanage which is to be under his supervision. When she naturally wants to insure the orphanage against fire, Pastor Manders demurs, explaining that she would be showing a complete lack of faith in God. If His eye was on the sparrow, surely it would watch over such a charitable undertaking. Trust to the Providence of God and all will be well. Of course, the orphanage burns to the ground, as a result of Pastor Manders's mishandling of a candle.

Pastor Manders comes across as a pious fool, as Ibsen no doubt intended. Yet his trust in Divine Providence pales compared to that of Jonathan Edwards, a brilliant intellectual who devoted his life to the subtle intricacies of John Calvin's theology. One night the house belonging to a member of Edward's congregation burned to the ground. Several of the members' children were killed in the blaze. However, one child survived, whereupon Edward and the surviving members of the family held a special service of thanksgiving to God, for having spared the one child. Today, the idea of thanking God for not burning to death *all* our children is frankly incomprehensible.

Closely coupled with the doctrine of Divine Providence was the often-stated assertion that we are not privy to God's decisions or designs. As the English poet William Cowper famously put it: "God moves in a mysterious way, / His wonders to perform…" And if we did not get Cowper's message, the final stanza of the poem reads: "Blind unbelief is sure to err, / And scan his work in vain; / God is his own interpreter, / And he will make it plain."

Mere mortals cannot interpret God's plans. It is enough simply to leave history in His all-guiding hands. That God's justice will prevail in the end, however, is not a theory of history. It is simply a pious hope, predicated on faith in a loving and omnipotent God. It seeks to find no inherent pattern in secular history. Mankind may move forward a step or two, but these steps can be quickly erased by the all too human propensity to backslide, as the Baptists like to call it. Indeed, things may well get worse, terribly, fearfully worse, before the Second Coming. The only sure ground for optimism is that no matter how wicked human beings become, God will bring them to His justice in the end.

Yet it is all too easy to move from the pious hope of seeing God's justice on earth to the hubristic certitude that you and your like-minded friends were the agents through which such justice would be achieved. "Those who stand up for justice will always be on the right side of history," Dr. King once said, clearly meaning those who would stand up for his own idea of justice—at that time, the liberal and progressive idea of social justice. We have already seen how President Obama, who often quoted King, displayed absolute confidence that he was on history's right side, while his opponents and enemies were on the wrong side. The sleight-of-hand substitution of our own idea of justice—i.e., social justice—for God's idea of divine justice may well come about unconsciously, but it is a long way from the blind trust in God's Providence celebrated in Cowper's famous poem. For a devout Christian of Cowper's stamp, to assume that our own human idea of justice must also be God's smacks not just of hubris but of impiety as well.

Since the time of Martin Luther King, there have been a few more sleight-of-hand substitutions. For King, social justice meant *equality*. Today, however, it has come to be identified with *equity*—a word so closely akin to equality that many have naïvely taken it to mean the same thing. But equity is not a synonym for equality. It is its negation. In the sixties, liberals, like Dr. King, urged the equality of opportunity. Let the playing field be level. Give each person a chance to succeed, or to fail, through their own efforts. Today, however, progressives have abandoned this ideal and have replaced it with one that could not be more different. What the social justice warriors of today demand is not an *equal opportunity* for success, but *equal results* in its pursuit. Personal failure is no longer the individual's fault, but proof positive of the lack of social justice, of structural racism, or of some other factor for which society, and not the individual, is to blame.

True social justice, by this logic, requires a complete overhaul of the existing social order, a radical overturning of the status quo, indeed, a revolution. And who is better fit to lead this revolution than those on the right side of history? But up to this point, no revolution, however violent, has been able to alter human nature. Some people will work harder, some not at all. Some will be smarter, others less so. Some will just be luckier than others. The dream of equity, of flattening the bell curve, can only be achieved by abolishing man himself.

This revolutionary vision of social justice has its origins not in Cowper's pious trust in Providence, but in the secular visionaries of the nineteenth century, all of whom had abandoned the very notion of a God who shaped history, but who retained a thoroughly secularized substitute for providence. These visionaries taught that history itself had a pattern immanent to it. It was not shaped by the hand of God from above but by certain iron laws working within history itself. Discover these laws and you would be in a position to chart the moral arc of the universe with the precision of astronomers studying the orbits of planets. And, indeed, it was quickly discovered that this secular moral arc did in fact tend toward justice—justice, of course, as defined by the particular philosophical visionaries, all of whom agreed that history had a pattern, which was seen as an upward progression through different stages.

Thinkers as diverse as Adam Smith, Georg Wilhelm Friedrich Hegel, and Karl Marx all agreed that this was how history worked, though they were divided over how these stages were characterized, they were unanimous that the various stages could be ranked in ascending order of progress. Each stage was an improvement over the previous stage. With the advent of the Future Revolution of the nineteenth century, however, a new twist was added. In addition to the past stages of history, which had come and gone, there were to be new stages of history, which, although they had yet to come, were assumed to a marked improvement over the present stage. Most typically, the future stages of history would be some kind of socialist order, or, at the very least, periods in which men and women would enjoy greater personal liberty, prosperity, and happiness, while the social order itself would become more just, equitable, and harmonious.

The idea that progress meant moving to a future stage of history was a radical departure from the neoclassical idealization of antiquity that first emerged during the European Renaissance. The men of the Renaissance, if they saw a pattern in history, it was that mankind had already achieved its true Golden Age long ago, during the heyday of Greco-Roman antiquity. Since then, it had been downhill all the way. Renaissance thinkers were the first to despise their own past. The millennium that separated their own time from the fall of Rome they now called The Dark Ages, during which nothing of importance had been achieved. They even condemned the magnificent medieval cathedrals as hideous monuments to barbarian "Gothic" tastes, so different from the rectilinear perfection of Greek and Roman architecture admired and emulated by the men of the Renaissance. If these men had an ideal future in mind, it was the restoration of classical antiquity in both the arts and science. The Renaissance with its devotion to the neoclassical ideal was not looking forward, but backwards.

That this neoclassical ideal persisted up until the very end of the eighteenth century is evident in the immensely influential aesthetics of art historian and archaeologist Johann Joachim Winckelmann, who maintained that the Greeks had offered unsurpassable ideals for later artists to imitate. The originality that is today so highly valued—and perhaps overvalued—in the realm of art and literature would have shocked the neoclassical tastes of the eighteenth century.

The neoclassical ideal was also quite alive among eighteenth-century political thinkers. It was shared by the American and the French Revolutions, both of which modeled their new form of government on a highly idealized version of the Roman Republic. The Roman elite was made up of senators, so that was what the founding fathers elected to call the men who, in theory at least, would possess the wisdom and gravitas of Rome's senatorial class. The idea of a government ruled by a set of checks and balances was derived from a reading of the French philosopher Montesquieu, who himself had borrowed it from the Greek historian Polybius. Even the French revolutionaries who proclaimed the birth of their new republic to be the Year One were adorned in togas and modeled their behavior on the heroes of classical antiquity as described in Plutarch's histories of eminent men. This raises the question of whether the American and French revolutionaries were hoping to start a new epoch in history or simply were attempting to restore a long gone and highly romanticized past.

The visionaries of nineteenth century had little use for such faux antiquarianism, though, as we will see, a highly idealized image of ancient Sparta would continue to cast its spell on utopian socialists such as Charles Fourier and among the New England transcendentalists as well. But their main theme was progress, both progress in the past and even more progress in the future. Progress, in short, was the overall pattern of history itself.

The ancient world had no such notion of a pattern to history. Consider the case of Polybius, whose massive history undertook to chart the rise of the Roman Republic from a small city to mastery over the Mediterranean Basin, recounting how Rome had defeated and subjugated its mortal foe Carthage in a series of three wars, as well as Polybius's own hometown and the rest of the once independent but continually warring Greek city-states. This was history on the grandest scale, and in many ways Polybius strikes us as quite modern. To begin with, Polybius spends a lot of time criticizing and even insulting other historians, both past and present, with a caviling pedantry that wearies his readers, who regret that these passages have been preserved while the story of Carthage's final moments has been almost entirely lost. Almost nothing survives of the many Greek historians to whom he refers, but their mere names serve as a reminder of how lively and developed the study of history had become in the Hellenistic world. It is also beneficial to realize that, from quite early on, the writing of history was clearly a matter of intense controversy among those who dedicated themselves to examining it. The fact that the works of so many ancient historians have been lost should not deceive us into thinking that the story told us by those who survived is the only way the story could have been told.

But did Polybius find any significant pattern in his narrative of Rome's fabulous accomplishments? Did he think that Romans were on the right side of history, or perhaps that their colossal triumph marked the end of history? Not at all. To see this, we need only to recall the words with which Polybius prefaces his ambitious undertaking:

> Now my history possesses a certain distinctive quality
> which is related to the spirit of the times in which we
> live, and it is this. Just as *Fortune* has steered almost
> all the affairs of the world in one direction and *forced*
> them to converge upon one and the same goal [i.e.,
> the triumph of Rome], so it is the task of the historian
> to present to his readers under one synoptical view
> the process she [i.e., *Fortune*] has accomplished this
> grand design.

The word that I have put in italics, *Fortune*, is obviously related to the Latin word *fortunata*, which in turn is a translation of the Greek term that Polybius uses in the original text, *Tyche* (Τύχη). Tyche is also the name of a Greek goddess, which is why the female pronoun *she* appears in the above quote, all of which leads us to ask the question: What happened to our supposedly modern historian Polybius? Did he really believe that behind the scenes of all the great historical events encompassed in his book there stands the figure of the notoriously capricious goddess, Tyche, spinning her wheel of fortune to decide the destiny of the world?

In fact, he did. Just as no pattern could be discerned in a random spinning of a wheel of future, or the throw of dice, or in any other game of chance, so too no pattern was to be found in history. Therefore, any search for it would have been as hopeless as the inveterate gambler's wishful schemes to "beat the house." Saint Augustine's idea of Divine Providence suffered from this problem. It might be true that history was in the hands of God, but no mortal could divine beforehand how He would act, though it was pious to assume that whatever He elected to do was for the best. But this did not make the course of history any more predictable than it had been under the fickle thumb of Tyche. But there was no need to evoke either God or goddess to introduce unpredictably into history—plain old chance was enough.

An offshoot of the chance theory of history came into vogue with the writings of the Scottish thinker Thomas Carlyle, for whom history was largely shaped by the actions of Great Men, heroes who soared above their contemporaries: Alexander the Great, Julius Caesar, Mohammed, Frederick the Great, and Napoleon, among other candidates. Yet, despite their world-shaking significance, the appearance of such Great Men was left entirely to chance. True, the historical circumstance must be ripe for their appearance on the world stage, but these circumstances do not create them. Perhaps a Great Man in charge of the Byzantine Empire in the final decades might have thwarted the conquest of Mehmed II, another Great Man candidate, but none appeared.

There is another and perhaps even more disturbing version of the chance theory of history, the antithesis of Carlyle's: what might be dubbed the "Insignificant Man" theory of history. Gavrilo Princip was a nineteen-year-old nobody when he assassinated Archduke Franz Ferdinand in Sarajevo on July 28, 1914, yet can anyone doubt that few events have had a greater impact on history? His one act, which took only a few seconds, set off a fatal chain reaction that eventually engulfed Europe and the world in history's most devastating war up to that time, which in turn permitted the Bolsheviks under Lenin to seize power in Russia, and which ended in a treaty that sowed the seeds of another world war, unleashing consequences still felt today. Who likes to think that the act of a complete nonentity was ultimately responsible for much of the ravaged twentieth century? A similar logic drives those who refuse to consider that otherwise utterly insignificant Lee Harvey Oswald could have been the sole assassin of a beloved president, John F. Kennedy.

The Insignificant Man theory of history may be distasteful, even repellant, but it should be sobering to all who believe that the march of history is inevitable and irresistible, to all who are certain that they are on the right side of history and have utter assurance about man's future destiny. Likewise, those who prefer to think of history as the outcome of impersonal forces, vast and tectonic, would be well-advised to recall the old adage about how "for want of a nail…the battle was lost" or Pascal's celebrated quip about the length of Cleopatra's nose. The course of history has repeatedly pivoted on mere trivialities, and there is no assurance that it will not do so again and again.

The chance theory of history cast such a powerful spell on the minds of European thinkers that it was not until the eighteenth century that someone came along who believed that he had found such a pattern: Giambattista Vico. Due to his relative obscurity, his writings remained largely unknown to the educated world, but he was not the first heavy-duty thinker to come up with such an idea. The Arabic polymath Ibn Khaldun had presaged Vico's ideas by nearly five centuries. His work would not be introduced to the West until 1697, Vico having developed his own ideas independently of Ibn Khaldun.

For both Ibn Khaldun and Vico, history was not linear but cyclical. This was a challenge to the view of history that would be introduced during the European Enlightenment, when a handful of visionary thinkers began to look forward to a future that would be better and brighter than the past. By the nineteenth century, the idea of progress, inevitable and unstoppable, would become the default mode of a variety of different thinkers. In contrast, both Ibn Khaldun and Vico argued that all societies, including their own, were inexorably doomed. Like the men who composed them, they too were born, passed through adolescence, and achieved adult maturity, only to face eventual decline and death. Furthermore, the men and women who lived during one period of these historical cycles had values, ideas, customs, and institutions that were unique to them and often incomprehensible, if not utterly repugnant, to those who lived in other periods of the cycle—in which case, who is to judge which were the best? Vico opened the door to historical relativism and an intellectual revolution commenced.

Giambattista Vico was born in Naples in 1668 and trained as a lawyer, though his real interest lay elsewhere. His book *New Science*, published in 1725, received little attention at the time, and today his fame rests on a revival of interest in his works by thinkers as various as Montesquieu, Marx, James Joyce, Isaiah Berlin, and Edward Said. Today, he has even become trendy in academic circles, perhaps due to the postmodernist flavor of his writings. At the same time, there are many features of Vico's thinking that hark back to the past. He did not challenge the view that human beings first appeared in the Garden of Eden not so long ago. Like many other Christian thinkers of his time, the discovery in the New World of Aboriginal peoples who were neither pastoralists nor agriculturists represented a challenge to the biblical account of the first human beings, whose sons Abel and Cain immediately took up the careers, respectively, of herdsman and farmer. Where did the hunter-gatherers of the New World fit into the biblical scheme?

Vico answered that these tribes had once been at a higher stage of civilization but had degenerated over time into the stage of savagery. It is possible that Vico may have offered this as an ad hoc explanation in order not to run afoul of the Inquisition, which was active in the Naples of his time. It is often suggested that this prudent fear was also responsible for his decision to treat the history of the Hebrews as *sui generis*, and thus exempt from the otherwise universal laws of history that it was the purpose of his *New Science* to elaborate.

Aside from the Hebrews, Vico held that all nations without exception must pass through a cycle of three ages, which he called *ricorso*. These were the Age of Gods, the Age of Heroes, and the Age of Men. Vico spends much time offering detailed explanations of how each age is different from the others, but instead of focusing on how they differ in material culture or in their mastery of technology, as we are apt to do, he is more interested in how the people of each age *imagined* their world.

The job of the archaeologist is to try to reconstruct societies and cultures of the past by bringing to light the material artifacts that they left behind. Their goal is to permit us to see how people dressed, what food they ate, what utensils and weapons they used, and what kind of habitations they built. A perfect reconstruction of a given period of the past would allow us to glimpse with our own eyes an actual moment of their daily lives, down to the last detail, but it could tell us little or nothing about how these people imagined the world around them. It would give us no clue about their idea of the cosmos, their sense of history or time, the stories they told of their past, or the futures they imagined for themselves both as individuals and as communities.

To grasp the mental world of an ancient people, we must look at the products of their imagination they left behind. This requires a different kind of archaeology, one that shifts through the different layers of the past, looking not for material objects but for their meaning. These would include the painted decorations on Greek vases, or the great stone calendars left behind by the Mayans, or the enormous stone heads on Easter Island. Some of these would be easier to decipher than others: it is clear what those frisky Greeks were up to, judging from the sexual antics depicted on their dinnerware, but scholars are still speculating about the blank stares of the huge monoliths on Easter Island.

By far the best way to enter the imaginative universe of an ancient people is to learn about the stories they told themselves: their myths and legends, their fables and sacred writings, their poetry and epics—all of which later critical historians simply dismissed as fabrications, as made-up tales. Vico did not take these products of the ancient imagination literally, but he felt there was a kernel of genuine historical truth behind them, however garbled they may have been after centuries of retelling. But, more importantly, he felt that the accusation that they were merely "made up," and therefore should be ignored as evidence, to be wrong-headed. Nowhere is this clearer than in his comment that, although the Trojan War "marks a famous epoch in history, it never in the world took place." How people imagine their past can have just as great an impact on history as how people imagine their futures.

According to Vico, the fact that all these stories and myths had been made up by ancient peoples offered the historian the key to understanding their world as they had imagined it. Why, after all, had they created these specific stories rather than others? Furthermore, because these stories had been made up by human beings, we were in a better position to understand them than we could ever hope to understand the natural world.

This ease of comprehension, however, disappears when we turn to the imaginative works of the distant past and of a different culture. Let us take as our example, Achilles, as portrayed in *The Iliad*. Within the context of the epic, it is blazingly obvious to the reader that Achilles is being held up for universal admiration as the very model of a Greek hero. If we dip a little deeper into Greek history, we learn that when Alexander the Great began his conquest of Persia, he kept his copy of Homer's *Iliad* by his side, and tried both to imitate and emulate Achilles in every way possible. Just as Achilles had his bosom friend Patroclus, so Alexander had his Hephaestion. Nor was Alexander unique. The Greek system of educating their boys was largely based on the reading of Homer's epics, and few, if any, ever came away thinking that Achilles was anything but a shining example of the true hero.

Today, readers of *The Iliad* find this adulation of Achilles hard to swallow. By our standards, he comes off as a pouting, spoiled, vicious bully. And what's up with him and his pal Patroclus? Are they gay? There are many other characters in the epic where our emotional response to them does not pose a problem. We feel the nobility of Hector and the pathos of his beloved wife, Andromache, which is why most of us are appalled when

Achilles drags the dead body of Hector around Troy, in revenge for his killing of Patroclus.

When nineteenth-century German theologian Friedrich Schleiermacher began translating Plato into modern German, he soon recognized the challenge of making the ancient Greeks, with their often shockingly different customs, such as pederasty, comprehensible to readers of his own age. The word he coined for the challenge of translating between cultures was *hermeneutics*, derived from the Greek god Hermes, who was the messenger the gods used whenever they wanted to converse. Some of these interpretative challenges, however, are more daunting than others. We feel that the Greeks responded emotionally to Andromache as we do, but their response to Achilles is so different from our own that the challenge seems almost insurmountable. A cultural barrier stands between the ancient Greek attitude to Achilles and our own, which raises the question of whether the hermeneutical project might not be doomed from the very start. If we cannot feel the same admiration for Achilles as the ancient Greeks felt, can we really hope to understand the ancient Greeks themselves?

In the instance of Achilles, if we're not confronted with a brick wall, we're at least facing what might be dubbed the "Hermeneutical Hurdle." This is what we encounter when we confront an imaginative product from the past—be it a myth, a poem, or a piece of sculpture—where our response to it is radically different from the response of its original audience, and, equally important, where we also *know* that it is different. There is, in other words, no Hermeneutical Hurdle if you are unaware that your response is different from that of those for whom the work was first created.

Much of the past confronts us today with the Hermeneutical Hurdle but there is another way of dealing with the past, once we have grasped just how remote it is from us: use precisely those aspects of it that shock us the most as the key to decipher the rest of their universe. Most often, as it turns out, this key has to do with the very different way they saw their future compared to the way we see our own, and this is especially true of the Greek hero.

Take the average man from all different periods of history and you will find, not unreasonably, a man whose main concern with the future is to keep it going as long as he possibly can. Chief among his concerns, he is anxious to preserve his own life, without which nothing else can possibly matter. For the sake of staying alive, men have even sold themselves and their family into slavery. But this is not the attitude toward the future that the hero must take. He may value his future life, but there is something that he values even more: his personal honor.

This in itself is a stumbling block to many of us, because we simply do not see the point of honor. It is one of those old-fashioned values whose merit we even suspect. We know of societies in which men will kill their own daughters out of a duty to preserve their own honor or that of their families. We know too that in the not-so-distant past, gentlemen would be expected to fight duels to defend their honor, and that to refuse to do would be considered disgraceful. Today, a challenge to a duel would only be taken as a bad joke.

Our current attitude suggests that we are definitely missing something about the Greek sense of honor, and that is the fact that their idea of honor was deeply embedded in their unique notions of futurity. Honor was due only to the hero who was able to risk his death for its own sake. He had to be prepared to give up his earthly future for the sake of a different kind of future. He was willing to die, not because he expected to enter Valhalla or the Islamic paradise, since the Greek hero knew nothing of either. Instead, he would die in order that men should praise him in the future—not his future but theirs—for what he craves is immortal fame, to be celebrated after his death.

Achilles's mother was the demigod Thetis, who had given her son a choice: he could live a short but glorious life by remaining to fight in Troy, or he could return to his home in Greece and live a long life in complete obscurity. Achilles chooses the short life of a hero over the long one of a nobody, to be rewarded with everlasting glory. Thetis doesn't mention it, but he will be the subject of the world's first truly great work of literature, *The Iliad*, and in the year 2004 AD he will be the star of a Hollywood epic, played by a barbarian born in lands unheard of: the handsome and dashing Brad Pitt. Three thousand years of continuous glory is as close to immortal as anyone can hope to get.

Greek schoolboys did not need to see the movie; they had *The Iliad*, and that was enough. Who would not aspire to be the subject of such an epic? Yes, Achilles had his flaws: his pride, his pouting, his passionate friendship, his colossal wrath, his over-the-top revenge. But these are the precisely the things that make him memorable—indeed, impossible to forget. No one has ever confused him with another character in *The Iliad*. Like King David in the Bible, it is not because he is the Boy Scout model of good behavior that he has lingered for so long in the collective memory of mankind. He is the eternal Bad Boy—preening, reckless, and irresistible.

Achilles does not die in *The Iliad*. Accounts of his death vary, but all agree that he was killed by Paris, the abductor of Helen, the prince who ignited the chain of events that led to the Trojan War. Yet Achilles returns to make a cameo appearance in Homer's second epic. When Odysseus enters the underworld in Book XI of *The Odyssey*, he encounters the shade of Achilles there. He is the king of this dismal and shadowy domain because of the great glory he earned in his brief life, but he is miserable in the underworld. When Odysseus tries to console him, Achilles replies: "Glorious Odysseus: don't try to reconcile me to my dying. I'd rather serve as another man's laborer, as a poor peasant without land, and be alive on Earth, than be lord of all the lifeless dead."

It is often speculated that *The Odyssey* was written after *The Iliad*, and it is difficult, recalling Achilles's lament, not to detect in it a critique, if not an outright rejection, of the central ethos of *The Iliad*, namely that nothing should deter one from the pursuit of heroic glory, and certainly nothing so trivial as the desire for a longer life. It sounds very much as if Achilles, whose praises were already being sung by the living, is regretting not having taken his mother's offer to go back to his home to die. If Achilles does not find his own immense posthumous glory enough to satisfy him, who else can ever hope to? It is as if Dante, when he finally ascended into Paradise on the last stage of his journey, had found all the saints sitting around, complaining that they did not live it up more on earth while they still had the chance.

Odysseus, let us recall, did not want to fight against the Trojans. He just wanted to stay home, on his island of Ithaca, as any sensible man would, with his wife and young son. When the other Greeks came to draft him into their crusade against Troy, Odysseus, a cunning man, feigned madness by yoking together a horse and an ass and then commencing to sow his fields with salt. Unfortunately, it was precisely because the Greeks knew Odysseus to be so cunning that they had come to the island, and his ruse was soon suspected by Palamedes, also a clever man, who is reputed to have invented dice. Taking up the infant Telemachus, Palamedes placed him in the furrow that his father was about to plow over with his wild team. When Odysseus stopped immediately, the game was up.

The Greeks were wise to take him along, however unwillingly he might have been. If there is one tale from ancient Greece that everyone knows, it is the story of the Trojan horse, the most magnificent act of lowdown treachery and deception ever recorded, and Odysseus was the one who came up with this ingenious trick. And why? To stop the endless fighting and to get back home to Ithaca. He did not seek the short life and posthumous fame that the true hero, Achilles, had chosen. He wanted the long life of peaceful and inglorious obscurity that Achilles had rejected. And in his visit to the underworld, it is none other than Achilles who tells Odysseus that he was right all along: The pursuit of glory after death, the aim of the hero, is not worth it. It is a delusion. Do not let the phantom of posthumous fame delude you; your future is *here*, on earth: make the best of it, even if it is short.

The *Iliad* is characteristic of what Vico calls the Age of Gods, in which humans used metaphor to make sense of the phenomena around them. The gods were invoked to explain the cause of things, especially those events that were unexpected and frightening. Evils such as plague and earthquakes were the result of divine wrath, which naturally required the performance of expiatory rituals. The Roman college of augurs had been established for just this purpose. In order to discover the best means of placating the gods, the augurs dutifully examined the inner organs of birds or observed the feeding habits of the sacred chickens. Divine too is the origin of the laws, all of which are attributed to semi-legendary sages whose wisdom surpasses those of mere mortals, and whose fiat alone decides what these laws should be.

Vico's second age belonged to a warrior aristocracy, where the ruling elite could justly claim to be superior by nature due to their manly courage, in contrast to the easily cowed, vulgar masses. Yet in Rome, it was also the age of the Conflict of the Orders, where the aristocratic patricians had to struggle incessantly with the plebs. One of the curious features of this conflict was that when the plebs, after much ado, were at last given the right to have a say in choosing one of Rome's two consuls, both consulships tended to remain in the hands of a few select ancient families, suggesting that it was not only the aristocrats who thought they were the cream of the crop, but that this was a near universal sentiment among the masses as well.

Perhaps the hallmark of a truly aristocratic age is when the claims of the aristocrats are generally accepted at face value, and no one is disturbed that there are two different sets of rules, customs, and even laws, one governing the aristocrats and the other their inferiors. In the rules that dealt with dueling, up until the nineteenth century, for example, only gentlemen could partake of this honorable institution. If a mere manual laborer insulted a duke on the public streets, the latter would settle the manner by having his footmen beat the culprit to a pulp, but it would be beneath his dignity to challenge the man to a duel. It is no wonder that during the second age, the aristocrats were accustomed to keep their inferiors in the dark by holding that the law was too sacred to be broadcast to the masses.

But above all, the second age is that of heroes, who, like Achilles, when given the choice between a good, safe life and posthumous glory, unhesitatingly choose the latter. Furthermore, in *The Iliad*, the Homeric heroes are so fascinating and admirable that the Olympian gods take interest in them and their fate. Athena looks after Odysseus, while the sea god Poseidon hates him for having killed his son, Polyphemus—the cyclops who trapped Odysseus and his crew in a cave in preparation for becoming his next week's meals.

Odysseus is something of the adult in a room full of adolescent boys. If he has ever felt the urge to do feats of daring just to prove he could, he has long outgrown it. He is also a man who uses his brains, for whom thinking and reflecting are critical, and it is precisely this faculty that brought the Trojan War to a finish. It is also of service during his long voyage home, where he also has to resort to deception, craft, and trickery in order to achieve his goal.

He finds his house full of drunken and oversexed suitors, all desirous of winning the hand of his faithful wife Penelope, as much for her property as for her beauty. Her suitors tell her that the husband for whose return she has been patiently waiting, has long since died in some remote corner of the world and that it is high time for her to marry again. After the ten years Odysseus had spent at the siege of Troy, a further ten years has passed, and no one has heard a word from the fabled man of many tricks.

Penelope, fortunately, has a trick of her own. She keeps putting off the suitors' importunate demands by a ruse. She explains that she must first finish the shroud for the eventual funeral of Laertes, the still-living father of Odysseus. Each day she works on it, while each night she unravels the work she has done during the day. For three years the suitors curiously fail to see through her deception, but they are all having such a marvelous time feasting on her cattle, guzzling her wine, and playing hanky-panky with her traitorous female servants that perhaps they could have cared less.

Sizing up the situation on his return to Ithaca, Odysseus pretends to be a frail old wandering beggar. His disguise is so good that only his old dog and old nurse recognize him, the latter after noticing a scar on his thigh while bathing him. He is scorned and scoffed at by the suitors, especially when he picks up the huge bow that the fabled Odysseus had left behind in the great hall of the house. All the suitors have tried their hand at bending the bow, but none have succeeded. And what could be funnier, they all agree, than letting the pitiful old man see if his enfeebled hands can string the bow? Within minutes, all the suitors lie dead in the great hall, the arrows of Odysseus having slaughtered them one by one. Quickly, he rounds up the terrified maids. Taking a strong rope, Odysseus ties one end of it to the wall, then strings a loop of it around each of their necks. Lifting the rope high on the opposite wall, he hangs them all in one fell swoop.

Are we still in the Age of Heroes? No, we have clearly moved on to the next stage, the Age of Men, when it is cool reflection and not reckless bravado that wins the day. Vico had his own theory about the epics that had traditionally been ascribed to a single blind poet named Homer. Anticipating what would become the standard interpretation of Homer in the twentieth century, Vico argued that the poems arose out of an oral tradition in which many individual poets participated collectively. Not only was the Trojan War a fiction, but so was Homer himself. At the same time, Vico believed that *The Iliad* was the work of a young Homer—that is, a poem created by an earlier set of poets—while *The Odyssey* was the work of an old Homer—meaning that it was the product of a later age that, as we have seen, had clearly begun to have its doubts about the heroic ethos unapologetically celebrated in *The Iliad*. These doubts are entirely characteristic of Vico's third stage, the Age of Men, in which reflection has replaced the old heroics. The Trojan War did not end in one final glorious battle between two great heroes, but by a stratagem devised by the wily and brainy Odysseus, the paradigmatic embodiment of Vico's third stage.

The entire *Odyssey* is a celebration of this "man of many devices." Through his long and protracted voyage back to Ithaca, he repeatedly demonstrates his foresight, his cunning, and his power of reflection. Knowing the dangers that the songs of the Sirens posed to passing sailors, luring them to their death on the sharp rocks upon which they are perched, Odysseus devises a clever stratagem: he stuffs the ears of his crew with wax and cotton, rendering them insensible to the blandishments of the Sirens' lethal song.

Yet Odysseus must hear the Sirens himself. His thirst for knowledge, even dangerous knowledge, possesses him. This too is a characteristic of the third stage: the desire to know, no matter the cost. Aristotle, the preeminent philosopher of the age of reflection, begins his *Metaphysics* with the words: "All men by nature desire to know." But this was not even remotely true of the men in Vico's previous two stages, when even the concept of objective knowledge would have been incomprehensible, since it implied a distrust of mere opinion or received wisdom. In the third stage, on the other hand, knowledge was desired simply for its own sake, and even "forbidden" knowledge was not off limits, as Odysseus demonstrates when he insists that, alone among mortals, he will hear the Sirens' song and live to talk about it. Cunning, of course, is required. He has his sailors tie him firmly to the mast of their ship and commands them not to unbind him no matter how vehemently he implores them. And back home in Ithaca, it is once again no show of mere dim-witted bravado but Odysseus's craftiness that saves him, along with his beloved wife and son. What is most remarkable about Odysseus is not his courage but his capacity for foresight.

The new emphasis on foresight implies that many of the Greeks had come to think that maybe a long and uneventful life was not such a terrible fate after all. Wars would still have to be fought, but no longer by individual heroes pitting their personal prowess against each other. The key to victory now lay in organizing large groups of men, as the Spartans had done with the phalanx, a close-knit formation in which each individual had to become a living cog in a formidable war machine made of armor-clad bodies and long spears. Extensive practice was required to train the soldiers to move, turn around, and fight as a single unit. Iron discipline was the rule of the day, and nothing could be more undesirable than a soldier who decided to break ranks in order to become a hot-dogging hero. Collective discipline became the path to military success, along with military leaders who possessed foresight.

Foresight, in short, is the attempt to eliminate the element of surprise, both in battle and in ordinary life, though obviously this is a goal that is often missed. But foresight also has a political dimension. When a leader inherits his position, as a king or prince, obedience is owed to him by his followers based on who he is, not because of his personal qualifications. When the king is a fool, people are stuck with him, unless of course they kill him and replace him with another king, hoping the new one isn't a fool as well. When the leader is the best fighter with the greatest personal courage, there is a danger that his very audacity will lead him into rash and disastrous decisions, but in the age of reflection, people don't want a dashing hero who ends up leading them to a heroic last stand, but a sensible one who believes in living to fight another day. Naturally, they will also want the best man for the job, which means that it will be up to the people to decide who this man is (not all the people, of course, just those most respected and trusted—the basis of popular government).

In Vico's third age, there is the growing sense of human equality that marks the transition from aristocracy to popular government. There now develops a legal system in which all men, regardless of birth, rank, or economic status, possess the same standing under the law (at least in theory). These laws are now made public so that all can know both their rights and their duties. The wise legislator Solon, who had given Croesus his sound advice, had done exactly this when he devised a new set of laws to govern the unruly Athenians and then set them on public display so that all citizens would be informed of the laws under which they lived. At the same time, language loses the strain of heroic poetry and becomes merely a conventional means for communicating our prosy everyday thoughts, desires, and interests, serving merely utilitarian ends. In terms of Roman history, this was the period in which historians like Tacitus were no longer interested in embellishing the fables handed down by antiquity, as Livy had done, but in chronicling the very unheroic events of the recent past, often relying on materials from the period in question, such a memoirs, official documents, and earlier written histories.

But Vico's story does not stop at this third stage. There is also a fourth stage in the cycle, and this is one of decline, which Vico calls "the barbarism of reflection." Put into current terms, this occurs when the individuals of a society have lost any sense of their communal bonds and seek only their own narrow interests, without regard to the common good. Furthermore, their only guide to conduct becomes purely subjective; whatever feels good becomes the highest good. By this process, human beings begin to return to their original state of being: only a little above the beasts, self-seeking, and interested only in their own immediate and very personal futures. At this final stage, the collective concern for the long-term future of their society (characteristic of ancient Rome) vanishes, and with it, a total repudiation of the claims of tradition to be taken as social norms for the rising generation.

For Vico, the decline of a society begins when the human mind, having become addicted to rational inquiry and debate, gradually begins to lose its confidence in the capacity of reason to reach definite conclusions on any question, resulting in radical skepticism. In short, while some thinking may be good for you, too much is sure to be bad, if not to you personally, then to the society whose values you can no longer believe in. The barbarism of reflection is epitomized for Vico by the rise of those whom he calls "learned fools."

Looking around today at the many academics who have gone woke, we may be excused for wondering if we are not already well into Vico's fourth stage. When men and women with PhDs tell us, without blushing, that men can get pregnant, that mathematics is an instrument of white oppression, and that mastectomies performed on healthy twelve-year-old girls is "gender-affirming care," it is hard to avoid the impression that we are dealing with "the learned fools" of Vico's fourth stage, although it is hard to believe that the learned fools of early times were quite as smug as those who flourish today in the groves of academia. But this fourth stage, with its turn to utilitarianism, subjectivism, and hyperrationality, carries within it the seeds of its own destruction. It is of course possible that the fourth stage of history may be more prolonged for some societies than others, but none can be expected to be permanent. None can claim to represent the end of history, though it is usually at this stage that societies seem most tempted to believe that they have reached it.

Vico's cyclical view of history, if correct, also dooms all those who believe that it is possible to restore the virtues and glories of a past age once its term of existence has ended. Consider the famous case of Brutus and Cassius, who openly justified their assassination of Julius Caesar by declaring their intentions to return to the old ways of the Roman Republic, before it had become enmeshed in one bloody civil war after another. They failed, of course, but for Vico, this was only to be expected. The cycle of history moves inevitably forward; it cannot be put into reverse.

The dream of restoring an ideal past and the dream that we are heading toward an ideal future share a common feature: both assume there is an ideal of how mankind should live and act—an ideal set of laws, customs, institutions, morals, and conceptions of the universe. This ideal society presents a standard by which other periods of history can be judged. Though all fall short of its immaculate perfection, these periods can be ranked by how they compare to the ideal age—some falling far short, while others represent a progressive approximation to it. But where is the ideal society in Vico's vision of history? Each age has its own way of imagining the world, its own ideal set of laws, customs, institutions, and morals that often seem absurd and incomprehensible to the other ages.

We moderns are often horrified by what the Romans admired as virtues. Consider one of the more famous tales the Roman historian Livy recounts for us. In the fourth century BC, Titus Manlius Imperiosus Torquatus had achieved the unheard-of distinction of being chosen as consul in three different years, as well as dictator, also in three different years. During the campaign against a neighboring tribe called the Latins, Manlius and co-consul Publius Decius Mus decided that discipline among the Roman troops was getting slack, whereupon they reinstated the harsh policy that any man who left his post for any reason would be immediately condemned to death.

Meanwhile, Manlius's son, who was covetous of glory, like all Roman young men, saw an opportunity to obtain it. Accompanied by his friends, he broke ranks, charged at a contingent of Latins, and defeated them soundly, taking the spoils of war back to the two consuls. Roman soldiers did not snatch up the spoils of their defeated enemies for their own personal gain, as the barbarians did, but collected their loot together to be allocated fairly by their commanders according to merit. Here the son of Manlius was no doubt expecting to receive the praise due to his daring feat. Instead, to the horror of all who witnessed the scene, his father ordered the immediate execution of his son. The order was carried out and, as Livy reports, such strict adherence to the ancient virtues of Rome became known as "Manlian discipline."

During the French Revolution, Manlius became a hero again. Various French neoclassical painters made him the subject of their historical canvases, but most people today find the story absolutely appalling. But the Romans, in their turn, would be no less shocked by our reluctance even to discipline our own kids by an old-fashioned spanking. Which of us is right? Can we be fair judges of such a question, given that our own values are merely those prevailing in our own age? Besides, our own age can have no more claim to permanency or finality than any other, since, according to Vico, it too is doomed to pass away as all previous ages have done. Consider as well that it is only during the Age of Reflection that men come to champion such notions as objective truth, natural law, universal ethical principles—all concepts that were totally alien to the previous ages, in which right was simply determined by might, and every culture deemed its own ethos to be self-evidently correct simply because it was their own, while objective truth could make no sense whatsoever to those for whom the only truth was their own tradition.

Even to raise such questions in the eighteenth century was shocking, which no doubt explains that Vico's time would come only after Europeans had begun to wonder about the certainty of their own values, even to the point of embracing the notion of historical relativism and dismissing even the possibility of establishing objective and universal standards of right and wrong, truth and falsehood. Needless to say, Vico's theory was a direct challenge to his European contemporaries who made up the intellectual movement known as the Enlightenment, and who were not bothered by any question of historical relativity. They were all fully convinced that the age of superstition and ignorance was ending and that its crumbling remains simply needed to swept away, and as quickly as possible. Room had to be made for the triumphant entry of the Age of Reason: a new and powerful, lofty abstraction, always spelled with a capital *R*.

Yet like all the abstractions that men have held sacred, such as Justice, Equality, or Liberty, Reason proved to be extremely slippery. Different people may give lip service to the same sacred abstraction, but quarrel intensely over how to apply them in the affairs of everyday life. Two men suing each other both claim to be seeking justice in the abstract, but their own practical ideas of justices could not be more diametrically opposed. So too those who championed Reason in the abstract quickly came to bitter disagreements over how it was to be applied in practice. During the French Revolution, both the Girondists and the Jacobins claimed to be acting in the name of Reason. The Jacobins eventually won the argument, not by persuasion, but by the guillotine. That the Age of Reason culminated in such orgies of violence brings us to the question that we will address in the next chapter: Just how enlightened was the Enlightenment?

CHAPTER THREE

HOW ENLIGHTENED WAS
THE ENLIGHTENMENT?

Today, most people who think of themselves as progressive, and who have some knowledge of the history of ideas, consider themselves heirs to the European Enlightenment of the eighteenth century. But so too do virtually all who call themselves conservatives; they explain that they are adherents of the "good" Enlightenment that took place in Scotland during that century, often taking Adam Smith as their hero, while they denigrate the "bad" French Enlightenment, seeing Jean-Jacques Rousseau as their *bête noire*. This quite common attitude, however, ignores the fact that Adam Smith was a warm admirer of Rousseau and that—with the help of his close friend and follow Scotsman David Hume—he went to great trouble to bring Rousseau safely to the shores of England after the French philosopher and novelist had been hounded out of Europe. The generosity of both Smith and Hume in helping out the beleaguered Rousseau may be evidence of their good hearts, but it also indicative of the immense respect they had for Rousseau as a thinker, even a sage—a sentiment they shared with Allan Bloom, one of the foremost American conservative thinkers of the last century.

That American conservatives share many values of the European Enlightenment should come as no surprise. The American Revolution, the Declaration of Independence, and the writings of the United States Constitution were all the products of the Age of Reason, after all. The founding fathers were not interested in conserving the traditions of the Old World, but believed that they were establishing a new order appropriate to their New World, expressed in the Latin motto affixed on the reverse side of the Great Seal of the United States: *Novus ordo seclorum.* Less than two decades later, the French Revolution would take this conceit quite a few steps further, proclaiming the year 1792 to be Year One, as if history were making a fresh start. It didn't, of course, and Napoleon very sensibly abolished the revolutionary calendar on January 1, 1806.

During the Age of Reason, however, the position taken by conservatives at that time was emphatically opposed to the social and cultural innovations advocated by their enlightened contemporaries. And if we take political labels at their word, isn't that what conservatives should be doing: insisting on conserving the traditions of the past and opposing newfangled innovations as untried and therefore dangerous? Just as the temperamental progressive longs for change, the temperamental conservative is quite content to leave well enough alone—as the redneck bumper sticker asserts: "If it ain't broke, don't fix it."

For most of human history, the ordinary man and woman have been temperamental conservatives. The "Change We Need" slogan may work for us, but only a handful of cultures have ever felt the same way; for most, it would have been blasphemy. Change was dangerous. Change was unthinkable. Change was just plain bad. Charles Darwin noted that most of the "sports" randomly produced by nature—the freaks deviating from the biological norm—were doomed to vanish. If you were too freaky, you died. For most humans in the past, deviating from the norms laid down by tradition was no less threatening, and those who attempted it usually suffered the fate of the biological freak: they were eliminated, as was Socrates when he challenged the Greeks' traditional ideas about the gods.

When everyone in a society is a temperamental conservative, such an attitude is regarded as simply the natural order of the world—so obvious that no one even thinks about it. There is no need to defend it, because no one attacks it. But if you examine the various groups and individuals who call themselves conservatives in the United States today, you will quickly see that not a single one of them believes that everything right now is just the way it should be. On the contrary, each of them is convinced that things would be much better if they were able to make changes to the current status quo. The neoconservatives dream of bringing liberal democracy to the rest of the world. The libertarians want to do away with all laws that intervene with the individual's freedom to choose his own destiny. The nostalgia-drenched Make America Great Again movement, though more visceral than cerebral, wants to return to a long-past America. But what the new wave of American populists wishes to restore is the founders' concept of a minimalist government, derived from the hero of the Enlightenment, John Locke.

But if we are all children of the Enlightenment, today's progressives quite naturally believe they are its chosen heirs—the legitimate offspring of this movement. Today's modern atheists, with their evangelical mission to convert the world, also claim to be carrying forward the mission first initiated by the great Enlightenment thinkers such as Voltaire, Edward Gibbon, and David Hume (whose attacks on the Christian faith they are only taking to its logical conclusion).

Yet the one thing all sides agree upon is that the modern idea of progress was at the heart of the European Enlightenment. This, however, turns out to be a highly questionable claim. There was much that was radically new about the Enlightenment. Like the European Renaissance before it, it broke with many of the tenets that had dominated the thinking of Christendom for well over a millennium, offering up new ways of seeing the world and man's place in it—though many of these new ways were in fact revivals of ideas that had been current in classical antiquity.

The Renaissance took great pride in its claim to have brought about the revival of ancient learning. This rebirth (the literal meaning of *renaissance*) had brought with it a renewed interest in the various philosophies that had been current among the Greek and Roman elite, such as stoicism, epicureanism, and skepticism—all of which offered alternatives to the

Christian faith. Traces of these influences can be found mixed together in virtually all leading thinkers of the eighteenth century, but they do not explain what made the Enlightenment something absolutely new in the history of the human mind.

With few exceptions, the thinkers of the Renaissance uniformly believed that the last word on science was to be found in the writings of the ancients: physics in Aristotle, medicine in Galen, astronomy in Ptolemy, mathematics in Euclid. If you wished to learn about human anatomy, there was no need to examine a human corpse; it was enough to read Galen's writings. It took immense courage for rare heretics like Andreas Vesalius to believe that they could improve medical knowledge by actually dissecting and examining a human corpse. The idea that empirical inquiry was the foundation of science met stiff resistance from those who believed that all scientific questions had been adequately answered by the writers of antiquity.

The Copernican Revolution was not only attacked by the Roman Catholic Church but also by leading scientific figures, among them Danish observational astronomer Tycho Brahe, whose discovery of the supernova Tycho's Star, on November 11, 1572, led him to reject the Aristotelian-Ptolemaic belief that the heavenly stars were eternally fixed, immutable, unchanging. Yet the Copernican theory raised obvious questions that could not be answered by the physics of the time. If the earth revolved around the sun, it had to move at an unimaginable rate of speed. Why did we not feel this motion? How did we even manage not to be blown off into empty space?

It would require the development of an entirely new physics to solve these problems, beginning with Galileo and Kepler and receiving its consummation with Newton. Once Newton had been accepted—and this took considerable time—it appeared to all educated men and women that the last word had been said about the physical universe. No one doubted that Newton's theory represented a giant step forward, but no one doubted that it was also the final step. The idea that there could be future progress in our understanding of physics and the universe was unthinkable.

As Alexander Pope put it: "Nature, and nature's laws lay hid in night / God said, Let Newton be! And all was light." Yet Newton's theories, for all their revolutionary impact on science, did not challenge the still dominant Christian understanding of the universe. Newton followed the lead of Archbishop Ussher, who had calculated that the universe was created around 4000 BC, and by his own calculations, based on his reading of the book of Daniel, Newton determined that the universe would end sometime between 1948 and today.

There were also a number of external factors that played a role in the advent of the Enlightenment, such as the ascendency of Europe. For most of its history following the fall of the Roman Empire, Europe had no claim to represent a higher state of civilization than did the Chinese or the various Islamic civilizations, particularly the Ottoman Empire. Economically, materially, and militarily, they were pretty much operating at the same level, though the Ottoman armies often were more than a match for their European antagonists. Yet this changed dramatically around the sixteenth century, with a number of factors playing significant roles, such as the development of new economics, new technology—especially in navigation and warfare—and an increased rationalization of government administration. This marked advance over non-European civilizations was consolidated in the idea that Europe was "ahead" of other parts of the world. Comparatively speaking, Europe had made "progress," while the other civilizations were lagging behind. Few Europeans denied this fact, but explaining how it had come about was another matter. It was not until the nineteenth century that various European thinkers began to argue for a racial basis for their global supremacy, with consequences that are still felt today.

The Age of Discovery was perhaps an even more decisive factor in making Europe ripe for enlightenment. When European navigators sailed to the East Indies in search of fabled riches, they set off a chain reaction that would over time lead to European domination of the globe during the Age of Empire in the nineteenth century. Increased familiarity with India,

China, or Japan did not require a radical rethinking of human history; the discovery of the New World emphatically did.

In addition to rendering null and void the geography of the world as handed down by the ancients, the existence of the New World challenged what had previously been accepted by all Europeans with regard to the origin of the human race. Genesis had told of the creation of the first man, Adam, and his sons Cain and Abel. Cain invented agriculture, while his brother Abel was the first pastoralist. Prior to the discovery of the New World, Europeans were quite familiar with both modes of subsistence. Yet the New World was full of tribes that practiced neither farming nor the domestication and herding of animals. They were first called "savages," which originally meant "dwellers of the forest." Later they came to be called "hunter-gatherers."

How did these strange new beings fit into human history? Various European thinkers attempted to answer this question in different ways, yet the most influential response came from John Locke, who declared that in the beginning, everything was America—all mankind had originally been hunter-gatherers. From this thesis, the question naturally arose: How did human beings emerge from this primitive stage? This tantalizing question led to a proliferation of various conjectural histories, which attempted both to explain how humans developed and to present the distinct stages of this development. Adam Smith, as we will see in a later chapter, offered his own solution, laying the foundation for thinking about history as preceding through a set of stages, each one representing progress over the one before.

Through a combination of all these factors, a hitherto unprecedented attitude toward the future sprang into being with the Enlightenment. None of the classical philosophers had proposed an alternative to the standard model of historical, and even cosmic, degeneration that was the default assumption of thoughtful men in antiquity. The European Enlightenment, on the other hand, offered mankind the vision of a future that was better than the past, though much more tentatively than is sometimes supposed. What all the thinkers of the Enlightenment shared, on the other hand, was a rejection of tradition as the guide to the future, though most were less sanguine about the future than is generally supposed, given mankind's dismal track record in the past.

Most thinkers of the Enlightenment adhered to the venerable tradition that regarded human nature as fixed and immutable, and were thus inclined to pessimism. When Voltaire declared that history is only the register of crimes and misfortunes, did he really expect anything different from the future? Immanuel Kant held that human beings could slowly and gradually improve themselves, but nevertheless cautioned that "out of the crooked timber of humanity no straight thing could ever be made." On the other hand, a few thinkers emerged who looked upon human nature as malleable, believing that by changing laws, institutions, and methods of education, a new and improved humanity could be produced. It was from these optimists that the idea of progress would finally emerge.

The French author Charles Perrault, best-known today for his charming fairy tales, instigated the Enlightenment when he dared to argue the unheard-of notion that "the moderns" had surpassed "the ancients" in both art and literature. This raised the hackles of his neoclassical contemporaries, like Racine and Corneille. Between the death of Perrault in 1703 and the French Revolution, the attitude of European intellectuals toward man's future ranged from pessimism to perfectionism, with all manner of positions in between. Despite these differences, there was near unanimous agreement that there were certain fields where progress had undoubtedly been achieved.

Between the years 1751 and 1772, hundreds of learned authorities combined their efforts to produce the single most prodigious achievement of the European Enlightenment. Edited by Denis Diderot and Jean le Rond d'Alembert, the French *Encyclopédie* was published in twenty-eight heavily illustrated volumes. Unlike modern encyclopedias, it was not a reference book containing articles on virtually everything under the sun, including history, religion, biography, and geography, among other topics. Instead, according to its subtitle, it was a *Systematic Dictionary of the Sciences, Arts, and Crafts.* The emphasis on these fields of human endeavor was natural, given the fact that there had been remarkable progress in the previous century in all these areas—indeed, going back to Descartes's *Discourse on Method* published in 1637. This progress, however, came in precisely those fields of activity in which creative intellectuals were involved, which left open the question whether progress in these specific fields had done much, if anything, to improve the lives of ordinary men and women.

In 1750, a year before the publication of the first volume of the *Encyclopédie*, an obscure scribbler and amateur composer from Geneva had entered an essay into a literary contest that was being held by the Academy of Dijon, which had posed the question: Has the restoration of the arts and sciences contributed to the purification of morals?

There are a couple of puzzling things about this question. It does not refer to the *progress* of the arts and sciences, as might be supposed, but to their *restoration*. If we take this phrase seriously, this would imply that in the past, the arts and sciences had been flourishing just fine, but somehow they had been lost. The past implicitly invoked was that of classical antiquity, with the further implication that the improvements that had recently occurred in Europe did not surpass the achievements of Greece and Rome but merely restored them. Even in 1750, it was still possible to regard the progress made by the arts and sciences in the previous century as nothing more than a return to the ideals of the classical world, which in turn suggested that once these ideals had been fully restored, no more progress would be possible or even desirable.

The other curious feature of the Academy's question was that it assumed that the recent progress of the arts and sciences might not be good for humanity in general. Perhaps the Academy expected to be flooded with essays affirming that progress of the arts and sciences was a boon to humanity and that it had even improved the morals of the human race in general, but the phrasing of the contest question indicates some doubt about the matter. Indeed, if the Academy had been utterly convinced that such progress was a blessing to humanity, it is probable that the winner of the contest would have been an essay in support of this position.

It wasn't. The winning essay was submitted by Jean-Jacques Rousseau, who argued that there had been progress in the arts and sciences, but that this progress had actually corrupted the morals of those caught up in it. Such false progress had only created an overrefined civilization that was rotten to the core, and that more such progress could only make matters worse. True, Rousseau was a brilliant writer, which certainly worked in his favor, yet the fact that the Academy of Dijon awarded him its prize suggests that its learned members may also have harbored doubts about whether "progress" was an unqualified good. The subsequent enthusiasm for Rousseau that made his name famous throughout Europe is further evidence that he was not alone in wondering whether "modern" civilization was blessing or a curse. The craze to return to a simpler, less civilized age was known as Arcadianism, and it was a powerful challenge to those who looked forward to a brighter future as the result of ever more progress in the arts and sciences.

Among the Enlightenment thinkers who did not live to witness the French Revolution, unambiguous optimism about man's future is found among the lesser lights more than the famous names. The first and best known among these was Charles-Irénée Castel, known to history as the Abbé de Saint-Pierre. Born in 1658, he grew to manhood during the glory days of the Sun King and lived to be eighty-five. An aristocrat by birth, he was educated by the Jesuits. Too sickly to follow the military career befitting his blue blood, he became a priest, though this vocation did not prevent him from advocating ideas that were radical not only for their time but for several centuries to come.

In many ways, Saint-Pierre was the prototype of the progressive reformer of not only succeeding eras but even our own, and perhaps the very first man to advance a genuinely optimistic view of man's future. Both his virtues and his failings are significant, because they will also become the virtues and failings of progressive thinkers from his time up to our own, which alone makes him worthy of more detailed consideration.

In his book *The Idea of Progress*, J. B. Bury devotes a perceptive chapter to Saint-Pierre, finding much to admire in this curious figure who "devoted his life to making schemes for increasing human happiness," while acknowledging that many of Saint-Pierre's proposals were impractical and often even childishly naïve. Like many very bright people, Saint-Pierre believed that if an idea convinced him, it was bound to be equally convincing to everyone else. A case in point: After considering the position of the Catholic clergy, Saint-Pierre decided that priestly celibacy had been a ghastly mistake and had led to a multitude of social evils. The blindingly obvious solution (to him) was to let priests marry. Writing up his thesis in an essay, he sent it to Rome, confident that upon perusing it the Pope would instantly issue a papal bull in favor of Saint-Pierre's reforms. The bull never came.

If Saint-Pierre was naïve, it was not due to his youth. When he was in his early sixties, he accompanied the Cardinal de Polignac as his secretary to the peace conference at Utrecht, marking the end of the War of Spanish Succession. The year was 1712. In the midst of these protracted negotiations, Saint-Pierre developed the idea that would be most closely associated with his name and memory, and which would go on to have a long life of its own: perpetual peace, achieved through an organization of different nations all pledged to pursue only pacifist policies.

Saint-Pierre was not the first to come up with such a proposal. In 1623, one Émeric Crucé published his visionary plan for a concert of nations, entitled *The New Cyneas*. The various members of his peace league would pledge to resolve their conflicts through arbitration, not war. Membership was voluntary, and quite remarkably, Crucé hoped that the Ottoman Empire would join it as well. The organization would be located conveniently in Venice, with Europe to its west and the Ottoman Empire to its east. No concrete steps were ever taken to realize this scheme, and it certainly came at an inopportune time as nations were becoming more zealous of their own national sovereignty, France in particular. But Crucé seemed to be more impressed by another tendency of his age: the accelerating expansion of commerce. He himself advocated free trade and was among the very first to connect the development of commercial activity with the idea of progress. Economic ties among nations would, in the long run, diminish resorting to violence—also a central belief among the liberal reformers of the nineteenth century, including Jean-Joseph Benjamin-Constant, John Bright, and Richard Cobden.

Saint-Pierre probably did not know of Crucé's work, but he was far more interested in establishing perpetual peace than in getting the credit for the originality of the idea. In his treatises on the subject, Saint-Pierre carefully explained how his own scheme would be in the interests of everyone. Each nation would pledge to be content with their existing borders and would renounce war as an instrument of policy. Naturally, this would require establishing a Diet that would have sovereign power over all the nations that belonged to it, but Saint-Pierre had no doubts that that all nations would gladly forfeit control over their individual destiny after they had grasped the beauty of his plan.

This, of course, was precisely what no sovereign nation was willing to do. The two organizations that he is often credited with inspiring—the League of Nations and the United Nations—had the exact same problem. Today, many progressives continue to pin their hopes for the future on achieving "a world government," though no one has yet devised an argument that could convince sovereign nations to relinquish the right to make their own decisions on issues that matter deeply to them. In addition, there were (and still are) those who feared that such a world government could become an instrument of tyranny, and violently rejected the very idea of concentrating so much power in a single source of authority—and not without reason.

Yet the Abbé de Saint-Pierre also had a more practical side. Of the recent progress in the arts and sciences, he tended to champion those ideas that led to the development of useful inventions that helped ordinary human beings in the grind of their daily lives. Here too was another theme that would be taken up by later progressives: what English philosopher Jeremy Bentham called "utilitarianism." According to this point of view, the best way to increase the happiness of the majority was to provide them with things that were useful to them in their practical affairs. This concern with the material welfare of ordinary people is another characteristic that makes Saint-Pierre seem far ahead of his time. Yet in another way he was very much a man of his age, and this is most clearly demonstrated in his faith in the power of reason.

René Descartes is usually given the credit for being the first truly modern philosopher, breaking with the scholastic traditions that preceded him, which he did through a radical thought experiment. As he explains in *Discourse on Method*, he decided to doubt everything that he hitherto believed he knew. But in doubting everything, he discovers there is something he cannot doubt—namely the fact that he is doubting. And since doubting is thinking, Descartes concludes his reflections with one line of philosophy that nearly everyone knows: "I think, therefore I am."

This method has been variously called systematic doubt, methodic doubt, universal doubt, and hyperbolic doubt. But, as eighteenth-century Scottish philosopher Thomas Reid asked, is any of this *real* doubt? When people use the word *doubt* in ordinary speech, they apply it to those cases in which they are genuinely puzzled whether or not something is true. They hear someone tell what seems to them suspiciously like a tall tale, and they naturally doubt its veracity. You can only doubt, in this sense, when you are actually doubting, not merely pretending to doubt.

Thomas Reid was right: Descartes's technique of universal doubt was only a rhetorical pose after all. It had been deliberately designed as a neat way to abolish all traditional claims to knowledge that had been taken for granted in the past. It was a *selective* skepticism, aimed at sweeping away with a single stroke the scholastic philosophy of the Middle Ages, as well as the revival of Greek learning that was the central ambition of Renaissance thinkers.

Such selective skepticism was an obvious departure from the universal skepticism of the ancients. The Athenian philosopher Carneades, for example, had doubted everything: his universal skepticism led him to conclude that no form of knowledge was reliable. Descartes's selective skepticism, on the other hand, permitted him to nullify all of man's previous claims to knowledge, but only in order to erect his own philosophical system, which offered Descartes and his followers complete certainty about the nature of the world, of man, and of God—a conclusion as far removed from Carneades's universal skepticism as it was possible to get.

Carneades had doubted even reason itself. It was the very fact that Carneades could come up with reasons both for and against every philosophical position that led him to conclude that we could know nothing for sure. The Cartesian idea of reason, in sharp contrast, excluded the very possibility that reason could contradict itself. That would be as absurd as to suppose that mathematics could contradict itself. A brilliant mathematician, the inventor of analytic geometry, Descartes aspired to obtain for his philosophy the same degree of rigor and certitude that Euclid had given to geometry, thus providing a solid and sure foundation for a new kind of knowledge: one obtained solely through unaided efforts of human reason, with no need to appeal to ancient creeds or authoritative texts, whether those of Saint Thomas Aquinas or Aristotle. Descartes's grand project was to give the human mind a fresh start, unencumbered by the accumulated errors of the past—an audacious aspiration that would earn Descartes the title "father of modern philosophy."

The Cartesian approach to knowledge was widely shared by thinkers of the French Enlightenment, and explains why the eighteenth century is often called simply the Age of Reason. But where had this faith in reason come from? Certainly not from any of the religious traditions that were battling it out in Europe: Calvinism held human reason to have been corrupted by original sin, while the Roman Catholic Church, though it gave reason a role in theology, had zero interest in any project which assumed that reason alone was a sufficient foundation for all human knowledge.

Though the word *reason* was on every enlightened tongue, few took the time to decide whether they were all really talking about the same thing. For some thinkers of the eighteenth century, reason was the means by which mankind could make a fresh start, casting off the fetters of the past and creating a far better world by the application of rational planning. Reason was autonomous, and it could and ought to command our will and actions. It would be our guide in ethics and in politics. In short, reason was the key to a better future. Most of these optimists would have agreed with Saint-Pierre that the thinker responsible for inaugurating the Age of Reason with a capital *R* was René Descartes.

The new faith in Reason, established by Descartes, provided the inspiration for those eighteenth-century optimists who shared it, though they were well aware of the daunting task that faced anyone who hoped to bring the light of Reason to men in general, given their own perverse reluctance to abandon the fetters that chained them to the outmoded past. In order to liberate the bulk of mankind from the shackles of tradition, the thinkers of the Enlightenment found in Descartes the perfect weapon of attack: selective skepticism, used polemically—designed not to question Reason itself, of course, but to demolish those enemies of Reason who stood in the path of human progress.

One such enemy, beyond question, was superstition.

Like many other thinkers of the Enlightenment, Saint-Pierre used the word *superstition* as a substitute for *religion*, which was his real target. The reason for this circumlocution was obvious: it was dangerous to attack religion outright, and a great deal of discretion and tact was required in order not to fall afoul of ecclesiastic authority. For example, it was clearly off-limits to attack the miracles in the New Testament, but no one would quarrel with a good Catholic—an abbé, to boot—who wrote an attack on the absurd miracles that were believed by overly credulous Muslims, Protestants, and other heretics. The fact that these miracles were not much different—and sometimes even the same—as those believed by Roman Catholics did not appear to bother the church hierarchy, while the more acute readers had no difficulty seeing the abbé's real message.

Yet Saint-Pierre was not an atheist but a Deist. This was a popular theological position adopted during the Enlightenment. It held that there was a God who had created the universe, but once He had set the huge celestial machinery in motion, He did not feel any further need to interfere in it. Human beings were left to their own devices and could not expect that God would alter the course of nature simply for their sake. Miracles were definitely out. Jesus of Nazareth may have been an exceptionally virtuous and wise man, but he was not the Son of God, nor had he been sent to earth to save men's souls. Deism, in short, accepted God but denied the doctrine of Divine Providence—a radical innovation that eventually led to a bitter feud between the two most famous French thinkers of their era: Voltaire and Rousseau.

Saint-Pierre, however, went well beyond the narrow limits of Deism in continuing to believe in the immortality of the human soul, which he saw not only as true but as an immensely useful truth in promoting human happiness. For him, the best way to deal with the natural fear of death was not to tell them that such fear was foolish and ignoble, as the ancient Stoics had taught, but to give them a reason to hope for a better life in another world.

Like all the Deists of his age, however, Saint-Pierre felt that the ignorant credulity of the masses would continue to impede human progress unless it was stoutly combatted by education—a wholly new kind of education, based on reason alone. Furthermore, Saint-Pierre was far ahead of his time in proposing that this new style of education should be freely provided not only to all boys—a radical enough idea by itself—but also to all girls.

Traditionally, education was only for elites, and male elites at that. There were sound reasons for this. First of all, there was the belief that an education could only be useful for those whose vocations required them to know how to read and to write, such as the all-male clergy in the Middle Ages. Since most Europeans were peasants, no one gave any thought to providing them with the tools of literacy, which would only make them unhappy with their lot. This may sound cynical to us, but it was grounded in the universal belief that the social structure of European society could no more be altered than the course of the planets. It was not only immutable, but it represented God's intentions and even his providence. Only within the hierarchical structure of the Roman Catholic Church could a lad of a humble and unlettered background aspire to improve his social standing through his own intelligence and energy. Otherwise, Divine Providence had established a Great Chain of Being, where every rational entity had its allotted place, from angels down to the gnats and mosquitoes that (they believed) spontaneously arose out of slime and muck. It was this cosmic hierarchy that fixed each individual's place in the grand scheme of things, along with his specific rights and duties.

The second reason to limit the range of those to be educated was what we call the bell curve of human intelligence. Most people simply could not handle the demands of a higher education. It would be a waste of effort on the part of all concerned to try to teach Latin to a dunce. Even Voltaire, who is often seen as the chief spokesman for the French Enlightenment, wrote that higher education "was not for cobblers or kitchen maids."

Like many of the other prominent French *philosophes* of his era, Voltaire believed that it was hopeless to try to lift the ignorant masses out of their morass of vulgar superstitions by appealing to their reason. It would be different if all people, from the time they were children, had been educated by the enlightened elite to respect reason, but this was obviously not the case with the vast majority of Europeans, who had been taught to take a host of absurdities on blind faith. The problem faced by the enlightened elite in the eighteenth century is an eternal one: if progress can only come about when there is an enlightened majority, how do you deal with those who refuse to become, or are incapable of being, enlightened?

This quandary helps to explain one more puzzling aspect of the French Enlightenment, namely the faith it put in "enlightened despotism" as a way of achieving general human progress. The logic went like this: If there was to be any hope of future progress, it could only come about when the absolute monarchs of Europe began to heed the counsels of enlightened thinkers. Voltaire himself assiduously courted Frederick the Great, with the aim of bringing that august sovereign over to his own principles, but failed. Denis Diderot was to prove no more successful when, after moving to Saint Petersburg, he tried to enlighten the mind of Catherine the Great, who may well have felt that Diderot would have been wiser to sit at the feet of the ruler of the world's largest empire than to ask her to sit at his.

A cynic might wonder if Voltaire and Diderot, like many other intellectuals, both past and present, buttered up the mighty in order to enjoy the perks arising from their privileged access to the sources of real power. This may have played some part in the avidity with which Voltaire, Diderot, and others sought to ingratiate themselves with despots, but the real reason lay in their pessimistic assessment of those benighted masses whom they hoped to elevate. Only an absolute monarchy, with its panoply of options for compelling obedience, could hope to uproot the multitude of superstitions implanted in the peasant's mind through centuries of indoctrination in error.

No trust was placed in what John Stuart Mill, in the following century, called "the marketplace of ideas." They wanted no free exchange of opinions; the only objection they had to state censorship was when it was applied to their own writings, not their opponents'. The best guarantee of progress was for the state itself to champion the ideas cherished by the enlightened elite and to suppress those views opposed to them. Those who were incapable of heeding reason would have to be compelled by force to relinquish their absurd prejudices. Hence the need for "enlightened despots" to provide a better future for mankind: there were so many people who would have to be forced to be happy.

If this sounds like a foreshadowing of the totalitarian regimes of the twentieth century, there is a reason for it. These regimes also believed that they held the key to a better future and were willing to use the full power of the state in order to compel mass support for their goals, as we will see in a later chapter. Examine the propaganda posters of Soviet collective farmers or of National Socialist *Hitlerjugend*, and all you will see are happy, beaming faces. The exact same attitude has been embraced by many of today's progressives, who are quite open in their belief that parents should play no role in deciding what their children should be taught.

The idea that the state existed to make its citizens happy was born in the French Enlightenment, and would come to dominate the politics of the twentieth century, though in strikingly different ways. Underlying this concept, however, is a novel idea of happiness—one that would have struck all ancient philosophers as absolutely perverse. To them, happiness was not something that others could give you, and it certainly wasn't something the state should or could provide. Rather, it was something that the individual could only achieve by his own disciplined efforts.

Eudaimonia is the Greek term that Aristotle used to express what he considered to be man's highest good. Literally, it meant having a good (*eu*) spirit (*daimon*), though it has frequently been translated as "happiness." Our modern idea of happiness, however, is far too dependent on mere happenstance to convey Aristotle's meaning. Happiness is normally understood by us to refer to a passing emotional state. For example, a woman who is happy with a compliment paid to her by a friend may be miserable an hour later from a snide remark by her husband, whereas *eudaimonia* suggests more of a permanent orientation of temperament, what might be better expressed by the words *well-being* or even *flourishing*.

The French Enlightenment, however, gave a new twist to the old idea of *eudaimonia*. Whereas Aristotle thought it was the philosopher who had the best chance of obtaining *eudaimonia* through his moderation, self-control, equanimity, and wisdom, for Saint-Pierre and others of like mind, there was a kind of happiness that all could enjoy: pleasure. The identification of happiness with pleasure would be at the heart of Bentham's philosophy of utilitarianism, another nod in the direction of the future.

The emphasis placed here on human happiness is not apt to strike us today as much of a novelty. The American Declaration of Independence enshrined "the pursuit of happiness" among our inalienable rights, and Americans have been pursuing theirs ever since. But the Enlightenment of the eighteenth century had turned on its head the old pieties which held that each individual had been assigned by Providence to the particular station in which he had been born, and that his vocation while here on earth required him to do those duties assigned to him. Happiness, according to the traditional view, was what you received in the afterlife if you had carried out the obligations of your earthly assignment.

If pleasure is happiness, on the other hand, then happiness can be achieved in this world, on purely secular terms. Indeed, it was possible for a reformer like Saint-Pierre to envision a multitude of ways in which an enlightened state could alleviate the pain of its citizens and add immensely to their pleasure, thereby increasing the level of general happiness in the world—this world, not the next.

The new ethic of eudemonism was widely shared among the thinkers of the Enlightenment: the aim of all human activity, both individual and collective, was to provide people with as much happiness as possible. But in the age of absolute monarchs, the idea that the government should aim to promote the happiness of its citizens was startling. Previously, all that was required of a good government was to protect life and property. To ask the state to do more, and to initiate programs and reforms that would actually make its citizens happier, was the first glimmer of what became the progressive ideal: a government that takes as its mission *improving* the lives of ordinary men and women, not merely protecting them from harm by others.

This approach was very French, and it marked a departure from the principles of classical liberalism that English philosopher John Locke had established in 1689 in his *Second Treatise on Government*. Locke's ideal government would exercise only the minimal functions necessary to preserve stability and order: it had the duty to protect life, liberty, and property, but no obligation to improve the lives of its citizens—that was entirely left up to the citizens themselves.

The French preference for a more proactive government was not due to an ignorance of Locke's philosophy. On the contrary, that philosophy, with its emphasis on knowledge obtained through our five senses, had exercised a profound influence on eighteenth-century French thought. It gave the enlightened elite a powerful weapon with which to attack religious superstition and doctrinal obscurantism. By demanding evidence based on our sense experience, it exposed the baselessness of delusions founded on fantastic tales, such as those encountered in the more improbable legends of the church. It was entirely possible that Saint Denis of Paris, an early bishop, had been decapitated by the Romans. It was less plausible that he had calmly picked up his severed head, then walked several miles with it under his arm, while preaching sermons to the astonished Parisians. As the witty Marquise du Deffand remarked to her friend, the *philosophe* D'Alembert, in a letter written in 1763, "It was really the first step that counted."

Locke's defense of religious toleration was also admired, along with England's strange medley of different sects. In his *Letters on England*, Voltaire wrote with his typical blend of insight and cynicism, "If there were only one religion in England, there would be danger of tyranny; if there were two, they would cut each other's throats; but there are thirty, and they live happily together in peace."

This witticism helps to explain the French preference for a proactive government, provided that it follows the advice and counsel of the enlightened elite. The English had liberated themselves from the tyranny of a single religion, while the French had not. The Roman Catholic Church dominated French life to a degree that no mere English sect could ever hope to achieve. The only force powerful enough to combat it was the state, and it would have to be a state with vastly more resources than the minimal one championed by Locke—an absolute monarchy, in other words. Yet there were obviously limits to what even the most powerful state could do in order to bring enlightenment to the mass of ignorant adults, most of whom were simply too mired in their old ways to see even a glimmer of the light of reason. But their children could still be reached.

Optimism about the future of mankind was most prevalent among those thinkers who put immense faith in the malleability of human nature, as we are most susceptible to being molded when we are children. The IQ test had not yet been invented, and human intelligence was understood to be the natural outcome of education, not biology. Many of the Enlightenment thinkers were singularly free from the taint of racialism, for example, the belief that some races are more gifted by nature than others. They assumed that children of every color and ethnic background, if offered the proper education, would perform equally well.

In addition, Locke's theory of the mind suggested that we all start out equal—that is to say, equally ignorant. It was left entirely up to education to fill in the tabula rasa that was every newborn's mind. Although human beings appeared to display remarkable variations in intelligence, the bell curve was artificial, created by the gross inequalities of education available at that time. The new emphasis on the power of education to improve the human condition led naturally to the idea of universal education, provided free of charge by the state—one of our significant inheritances from the Age of the Enlightenment. We have even inherited the idea that an education that fails to make all children equally bright has somehow failed and should be fixed, an idea embodied in the No Child Left Behind policy enthusiastically adopted by both Democrats and Republicans (though the result of this project, like many other high-minded reforms, has been severely disappointing).

Naturally such an education would need to make a sharp break with what had passed for an education in the past. Prior to the Enlightenment, the most important function of education had been to pass on a society's traditional values, and not just in Europe. All over the world, wherever the younger generation was being taught by its elders, the aim of the process was to teach the young to honor and preserve the "timeless" values of their ancestors. Tradition was a sacred trust, which is why education was normally undertaken by priests, mandarins, rabbis, imams, monks, and ministers. The very last thing that such an education was expected to do was to teach the young to criticize the traditions they were being taught to revere.

In those cultures that have no idea of progress, and that even fear change, such a method of education made perfect sense. We have been raised to think that the goal of education is to prepare our children for the future, but in a society that imagines that the future will only be more of the past, the young only need to learn those skills already possessed by their parents, and to master only the knowledge accumulated for generations. Change was something that had to be sturdily girded against, not something to be ardently embraced.

As much as the leading figures of the Enlightenment might disagree on a host of different issues, all agreed that the traditional idea of education had to go. It was worse than merely useless; it was in fact responsible for holding mankind back. If there could be any hope for progress in the future, it would require an education that aimed at enlightenment.

The German philosopher Immanuel Kant offered a hint about what kind of education this might be in his essay "What is Enlightenment?" His answer is a two-word Latin admonition: *Sapere aude!* This can be translated several ways, but the one that suits our purpose best is: "Dare to think for yourself!" By this new standard, any education that deliberately aims at preventing you from thinking for yourself, by making you accept what those in authority want you to believe, is bad and should be abolished.

Yet if the solution is to dump the traditional goal of educating the young, what is to take its place? An alternative reading of *"Sapere aude!"* provides the answer: "Dare to use your own reason." The new system of education, rather than merely passing on the accumulated ignorance and prejudices from the hoary past, would now be based on reason. By this means, not only would the rising generation become disciples of Enlightenment, but the whole structure and order of society would be radically altered for the good. Mankind's future would henceforth be liberated from the shackles of the past. Instead of blindly following obsolete traditions, human beings could now take charge of their own destinies through the use of reason alone.

This all sounds very lofty, but in practice it becomes immediately obvious that reason has an odd way of meaning quite different things to different individuals. Martin Luther had told everyone who could read his German Bible to be his own priest and to make up his own mind about what the Bible meant. He was then shocked to discover that people came up with wildly different readings from what had seemed self-evident to him. Kant dared people to use their own reason and was puzzled to find that when people did, they came to conclusions different from his own. He lived long enough to see mayhem caused by the French Revolution when the Goddess of Reason (invoked to replace the God of the Bible) was devoutly worshipped by men who would soon fall to cutting each other's heads off, all in the name of Reason. Was this a problem due to bad reasoners, or was there something fishy about Reason itself?

Greek skepticism had long before warned that the only thing our reason demonstrated was that it could be used to demolish any argument, but universal skepticism hardly provided a solid foundation for the education of the young. A child taught to question everything would be impossible to teach. As Rousseau would put it in his own book on education, *Emile*, "If you could reason with a child, he would not be a child."

The pedagogical course that would be charted by the enlightened educators of eighteenth century would become the standard line taken by all future attempts to enlighten the children of benighted parents. It would urge the child to think critically about the traditions and beliefs of his parents, but to take on faith the views and opinions embraced by the educators themselves. Selective skepticism became a powerful weapon in the hands of those who wanted to subvert or even overthrow the accepted traditions of their society. Today, we can see it in action all around us, as woke educators challenge supposedly outdated facts in fields like biology and history.

Yet by its very nature, the preference for selective skepticism compromised the mission of the Enlightenment, since the intellectual energy that might have been employed in constructing a better future was largely engaged in attacking the institutions and traditions of the past. The essence of critical thinking, after all, is to refute and demolish, not to affirm and construct. What happens, however, when a traditional way of life is subjected to such attack?

First, there will be tremendous resistance to the attack. Most people will cling tenaciously to the traditions in which they have been raised. This will be true of any society, but especially those that have long-standing institutions, the purpose of which is to guard and preserve these traditions, and few have ever succeeded in doing this as well as the Roman Catholic Church. Armed with its own highly trained and intelligent defenders, the Catholic Church was not remotely interested in divesting itself from its ancient traditions in order to please a handful of impractical dreamers, as Saint-Pierre discovered when he recommended abolishing priestly celibacy. This made the task of bringing enlightenment to the masses appear hopeless to the would-be enlighteners, who then became increasingly pessimistic about human nature itself. But such pessimism was obviously incompatible with the starry-eyed vision of man's future that became pervasive in the nineteenth century.

Second, if the enlighteners succeed in disabusing the masses of their previous delusions, what would the enlighteners offer to them in place of their discarded tradition? A traditional way of life will always possess one singular advantage: no matter how silly or absurd it may seem, it provides a clear and unambiguous road map to guide us into the future. We know our role and the roles of others. We know what is permissible and what is taboo. We know what to do in unexpected situations. In short, abiding by a tradition is a way of lessening our natural anxiety about what the future holds, which explains why so many cultures of the past have fought tooth and nail to maintain their traditions intact.

The error of the Enlightenment was to see tradition from only one side: as a superseded relic of the past—when in fact tradition is a method of dealing with the future. Tradition offers a guidebook about what to do next in virtually any contingency. Because this guidebook had served them well in the past, it was deemed reliable for dealing with the future—and certainly more reliable than a plan that has never been tested, however sound in theory it might be. Indeed, the longer tradition had successfully guided a society through challenges to its survival, the greater the resistance to abandoning it. What the enlighteners see as a relic of the past, the traditionalists see as a time-tested chart with which to navigate the perils that have faced their society in the past and will do so in the future.

Critical reason can tear down a tradition, but what can it put in its place?

This question would simmer in treatises and pamphlets until the coming of the French Revolution, when the power of the revolutionary state was used to dismantle the institutions that had previously constituted an entire way of life. All the revolutionaries were students of the Enlightenment. All thought that Reason with a capital R could replace the traditions that had been swept away, but all soon discovered that in a national assembly there were as many reasons as there were members. Tradition, by its very nature, spoke with a single voice, Reason with a thousand. Even those who loathed a tradition never had any doubt what it demanded: the strait gate, or a straightjacket. But all knew how to play that game. The game of Reason had no rules; it was a free-for-all.

Once a traditional way of life has been abolished, how do you go about creating a new way of life? This was the challenge faced by the leaders of the French Revolution, who discovered that it is far easier to tear down than to build up. It was child's play to rename all the months with lovely new titles, and even to change the calendar year of 1789 to the new Year One, but their attempt to replace the God of Christianity in the popular mind with the Goddess of Reason was a failure. She was a chilly deity that no one warmed to.

Yet neither the failures nor the tumult of the French Revolution dampened the spirits of the true believers. On the contrary, the French Revolution unleased a radically new form of optimism embraced by genuinely utopian thinkers like William Godwin and the Marquis de Condorcet, both of whom were confident that mankind's future would be one of a progressive development toward perfection, not just for European intellectuals like themselves but for all mankind. This was a far cry from the timid optimism of Saint-Pierre, but it was to have immense historical influence.

Ironically, Condorcet ran afoul of the authorities of the French Revolution in April 1792, when he submitted his own proposal for an entirely new method of public education. It was to be entrusted to experts like himself (Condorcet was a brilliant mathematician), who would act as guardians of the Enlightenment and be answerable to neither the government nor the public. The scheme was rejected as being contrary to the Revolution's principle of egalitarianism and denounced as smacking too much of a revival of the hated aristocracy—in this case an aristocracy ruled by an intellectual elite. It probably didn't help that Condorcet was both the old-fashioned kind of aristocrat as well as one of the leading French savants of his era. Later, when Condorcet criticized the new Constitution of 1793, a warrant was issued for his arrest as a traitor. He managed to escape the guillotine for a while but was finally caught and put in a prison cell, where he died under circumstances that are still murky: either by his own hand or by an agent of the government. In 1795, the National Convention adopted his educational proposal.

Condorcet is often regarded as the last important figure of the French Enlightenment, but in fact he should be seen as the first of the nineteenth-century utopian thinkers. It is true that he drew together into his own system the various ideas of previous thinkers. Like Saint-Pierre, he believed that women should be educated. He even believed they should be allowed to vote. But none of the previous sages of the European Enlightenment had ever dare to conceive of a work like Condorcet's *Sketch for a Historical Picture of the Progress of the Human Spirit*, a book that he wrote while hiding out from the authorities.

English historian Edward Gibbon asserted in *The History of the Decline and Fall of the Roman Empire* that history is "little more than the register of the crimes, follies, and misfortunes of mankind." His contemporary, Voltaire, who had written his own superb *The Age of Louis XIV*, agreed, writing that "history is only a tableau of crimes and misfortunes" (*l'histoire n'est que le tableau des crimes et des malheurs*). The other eminent eighteenth-century historian, David Hume, would certainly have concurred—indeed, historical pessimism seemed to be an occupational hazard of eighteenth-century rationalist historians. Condorcet, however, looked at the past with a new perspective. He was aware of the misery and suffering mankind had endured through long centuries, but he also saw in the past clear traces of a progressive historical movement, with even a hint of dialectical materialism thrown in. He argued that with advances in education, of the kind he had himself proposed, human beings would not only continue to make progress in the future but would progress without limit. The uncivilized nations of the world, Condorcet opined, would quickly catch up with Europe simply by reading Descartes and other apostles of reason. Medicine would continually improve until human beings would no longer die of old age—though of course they were still liable to die by accident, murder, or suicide. (William Godwin also flirted with the old dream of human immortality, which has been traced all the way back to the epic of Gilgamesh.)

This was progress as no one before had ever imagined it. Although Condorcet's final treatise on the idea of progress was an example of Enlightenment thought, by the time the book was finally published in 1795, all the leading figures associated with the Enlightenment were dead: Saint-Pierre in 1743, Helvétius in 1771, Hume in 1776, Voltaire and Rousseau in 1778, de Condillac in 1780, Lessing in 1781, d'Alembert in 1783, Diderot in 1784, Baron Holbach in 1789, Edward Gibbon and Caesare Beccaria in 1794. Only Immanuel Kant was alive in 1795, but by then he had written his three great critiques. In short, by the time Condorcet's book saw the light of day, the Enlightenment was over.

There is a marked tendency among those who have taken general survey courses in history to associate the European Enlightenment of the eighteenth century with the modern idea of Progress with a capital P. But even our brief survey of this period is enough to dispel this illusion. True, there was a consensus that the arts and sciences had made progress, though there was a dispute about whether this progress had really benefitted mankind. Some, like Saint-Pierre, threw out vague ideas to improve human beings and their lot, most of which were utterly impractical, but no one dared to suggest that some such improvements were inevitable. Optimism about mankind's future was in short supply among the leading figures of the Enlightenment, and to see progress as "a central concern of Enlightenment thought" is an example of the tendency to modernize the thinkers of the past in order to make them fit our own preconceptions.

Condorcet's optimism would inspire much of the utopian dreams of the nineteenth century. It would become the central article of faith for all seekers of the new, for whom, despite his many quaint absurdities, Condorcet offered something important: the hope in a better world to come. If this sounds suspiciously like what Christians had traditionally believed, there is a reason for it. Indeed, the best way of understanding the appeal of Condorcet's radical optimism is to see it as a replacement for a lost faith—the once nearly universal faith in Divine Providence. From the time of Saint Augustine, the notion that God was not only guiding human history but guiding it for the best was central to the way Europeans looked at their future.

In his final treatise, Condorcet had restored what the earlier thinkers of the Enlightenment had taken away: their faith in the future, though the new faith proposed by Condorcet was based not on belief in God but in the perfectibility of mankind. Yet by giving people the assurance of a better future, Condorcet had given them back the hope that the leading figures of the Enlightenment had denied them. Even the Deists of the Enlightenment, like Saint-Pierre, rejected the idea of Divine Providence. The very logic of Deism precluded it: like a clockmaker, God had created the universe but then had left it to run by itself. At least the Deists believed that God had made a good clock, but there were those who disputed even this. Indeed, two of the leading figures of the Enlightenment, Voltaire and David Hume, argued that God couldn't even make a decent wristwatch.

The most famous work of literature to be produced during the French Enlightenment was also by far the most pessimistic book of its age—perhaps of any age—namely Voltaire's brilliant novella *Candide, or Optimism*. There is a famous backstory to Voltaire's decision to write such a scathing satire: it is said that when Voltaire heard about the devastating earthquake that hit Lisbon on November 1, 1755, killing thousands of innocent men, women, and children, his eyes were opened for the first time to the fact that this was not a perfect world. This is of course balderdash. Voltaire was around sixty years old at the time of the Lisbon earthquake. He had already written two superb books on history, including *The Age of Louis XIV*, and there were few men in Europe with a wider knowledge of the past. Can anyone believe that Voltaire was unaware that there had been terrible earthquakes in the past? Or devastating wars? Or plagues?

Candide was written by a man who had an axe to grind, to attack the Christian idea that Divine Providence governed the world by showing just how awful a place the world was. The story of the remarkably naïve Candide is made up of many rapidly changing episodes, wherein all the evils and ills that mankind inflicts, or is afflicted by, are paraded before the reader, from earthquakes to *autos de fe*, from syphilis to war crimes. The butt of Voltaire's satire is the tutor of the young Candide, Doctor Pangloss, who has taught him that this is the best of all possible worlds. This idea was not original to the dim brain of Pangloss, who is constantly portrayed as an utter fool, but is derived from the philosophy of Gottfried Wilhelm Leibniz, who was certainly not a fool. Leibniz had, after all, invented calculus independently of Isaac Newton and gave it the notational form that it still maintains today. How had such an intelligent man come up with such a patently absurd idea?

Leibniz was wrestling with the same problem that had disturbed the second-century Christian heretic Marcion of Sinope, the first person who set about creating a suitable canon of Christian writings. It consisted only of the Gospel of Luke and ten letters of the Apostle Paul. Marcion had rejected the Old Testament (the Tanakh) in its entirety, on the grounds that the Creator God of Genesis had made a world that was "very faulty and imperfect." He argued that a good and competent God could not and would not have created a universe with so much suffering and misery in it. Pondering this very challenging problem, Leibniz used his logical genius to try to come up with a solution to the dilemma. It was obvious, he argued, that God could not have created a universe that contained logical impossibilities. He could not have a made cosmos in which two plus two equaled three or five, nor could he have made square circles or circular squares. These were limits imposed on the omnipotence of God by the very nature of things. Some of these limits are obvious to us in our state of very incomplete knowledge—like square circles—but there are other limits that our finite mind cannot grasp. It was these limits, invisible to us, that put constraints on God's omnipotence. If we could see and know these invisible limits, we would understand that God had no choice but to create one of the universes that were possible, and that, being good, he naturally chose the best one.

A much blunter way of putting Leibniz's idea is to say that this universe, with all its ills and suffering, is the best that God could do, which, phrased in this manner, sounds not like optimism but blasphemy. Marcion could have said the exact same thing about his incompetent demiurge, who had bungled his job of creation. What saves Leibniz from heresy is his contention that what limits God's omnipotence is not a failing on His part but arises from the nature of what is possible. As he wrote, "Not all goods are compatible," meaning that certain goods, like an earth without earthquakes, had to be sacrificed to achieve some other good.

Leibniz was obviously trying to rescue the idea of Divine Providence through his ingenious concept of an infinitude of possible worlds, out of which God chose the best. But how good was this best? If God lacked the power to prevent earthquakes and tsunamis, plagues and famines, then why should we pray to Him? According to Saint Augustine's doctrine of Divine Providence, all such calamities were seen as just punishment for our sins, inflicted for our benefit by a loving God: the due chastisement of erring mortals. But in the eighteenth century, this too-tidy solution to the problem of evil was no longer convincing to those who had come to expect more from the deity. The rationalism of the era had made it impossible to conceive of a God who could indiscriminately punish the innocent along with the guilty; obviously earthquakes and plagues did not descend on the wicked alone, but maimed and killed both the infants and saints. How could a just God do such things? At best, Leibniz had proved that this was the least bad of all possible universes. But such an anemic defense of Divine Providence certainly showed that its old robust formulation was no longer tenable even among intellectuals like Leibniz, who clearly wanted to defend it.

As it turns out, however, Voltaire did not write *Candide* to attack Leibniz, or because he had just learned earthquakes often kill people. He wrote it as an attack on Jean-Jacques Rousseau, with whom he had exchanged a series of letters on the question of Divine Providence. Oddly enough, this was the same Rousseau who had dared to question whether civilization was a good thing, and who now, in his later years, dared to challenge one of the key themes of the Enlightenment: its repudiation of the doctrine of Divine Providence, one of the very few articles of faith on which all the different Christian churches and sects agreed.

It is true that jealous rivalry for the admiration of the literary world stirred in the souls of both Voltaire and Rousseau. They were by far the two most celebrated writers of their time, and both had flocks of ardent admirers, even semi-worshippers. But there was also a genuine conflict between the two on the question of Divine Providence. Take away this faith from average people, Rousseau argued, and what do they have left? Faith in Providence provided a source of hope in a world of struggles and hardships. What could replace it if it was lost?

In January 1766, Jean-Jacques Rousseau arrived in England. Threatened with persecution for his ideas, both in his native city of Geneva, Switzerland, and in France, he had been persuaded to cross the channel at the behest of the two most eminent figures of the Scottish Enlightenment: Adam Smith and David Hume. In fact, Hume had traveled to France in order to bring the world-famous Rousseau back to England, where the two lived together in Hume's home at Wooten in Staffordshire and later in London. Rousseau remained in England for sixteen months and hated every second of it. He did not like the English, nor their language, which he could not speak.

On the first night Rousseau spent on his way to England, he shared a bedroom at an inn with Hume. According to Rousseau's later account, Hume passed the whole night muttering the ominous words, *"J'ai Jean-Jacques Rousseau"* (I have Jean-Jacques Rousseau) over and over in his sleep. Clearly, Rousseau began to think, here was the sign that he was being freshly entrapped in a new conspiracy to persecute him, with Hume as the ringleader. The visit did not go well. A persecution mania is bad enough when its victim is not being persecuted, but Rousseau had been hounded out of Europe, where both he and his books were condemned—the latter often burned by the executioner in lieu of their absent author. Rousseau would suffer paranoid delusions for the remainder of his life, though he was still capable of writing beautifully and even wisely to the bitter end.

Rousseau's psychological issues turned Hume's act of generous benevolence into a domestic nightmare, but there was a deeper and genuinely philosophical conflict between the two men. In his novel on education, *Emile*, published in 1762, there is a long section called "The Creed of a Savoyard Priest." The creed confessed is certainly not orthodox by the standard of its time, but it contained a sustained defense of Divine Providence—the very position that had long been ridiculed by Voltaire in *Candide*.

The skepticism of Voltaire, however, was nothing compared to the skepticism of David Hume. No significant figure of the eighteenth century pushed skepticism to the extremes that Hume did. His was not the selective skepticism of Descartes but the universal skepticism of Carneades. Unlike the other thinkers of the Enlightenment, Hume did not see Reason with a capital *R* as the solution to all the problems that mankind faced. On the contrary, in his *Treatise on Human Nature*, published when he was twenty-six, he had written, "Reason is, and ought only to be the slave of the passions, and can never pretend to any other office than to serve and obey them." Though he died in 1776, some two decades before the French Revolution, he would hardly have been surprised to see the Goddess of Reason fail abjectly in her task of resolving the violent passions that had been excited since the fall of the Bastille.

What motivates human beings to action, according to Hume, is not our powers of reflection but our emotions. They are the true springs of all our undertakings. Reason cannot check or control our passions, nor should it even try to do so—a position that deliberately turned on its head the tradition of Stoic moral philosophy, which held that reason can, and ought to, control our passions. In making his bleak assessment of the power of reason, Hume was perhaps unconsciously influenced by the Calvinism in which he had been raised, with its doctrine of total depravity: it said that after his Fall, man's reason had ceased to be his guide and has become only the tool of his unruly emotions. But there was another influence on how Hume viewed the role of reason in human affairs, namely his study of history.

During his lifetime, the work that made David Hume both famous and wealthy was his multivolume *The History of England*, a bestseller at the time and still well worth reading. No one who studied England during the Protestant Reformation could avoid noticing the violence and mayhem caused by human passions when in the grip of religious fanaticism. Could anyone be unworldly enough to believe that this fevered religious agitation could be quieted by reasoning with those in its grip?

On the one hand, there had been an excess of what Hume called "enthusiasm" among the various Protestant sects, especially the Puritans, who came to power in England following the execution of King Charles I. In eighteenth-century polite discourse, the term *enthusiasm* was used with the modern meaning of "wild-eyed hysterical fanaticism." Cathedrals were sacked: altars hacked to pieces, stained-glass windows smashed. But the Roman Catholic Church had its own problem with what Hume called "superstition," definitely agreeing with Protestant critics of Catholicism, who perceived it as something of a hocus-pocus racket to dupe the ignorant masses.

Yet in making these charges against the two dominant creeds of Christian Europe, Hume never for a moment supposed that the solution was to turn everyone into atheists, or even skeptics like himself. (It is a matter of debate among scholars of Hume whether he was himself an atheist or merely a skeptic.) In his *History of England*, Hume in fact comes down on the side an established church, like the Church of England, which was a branch and extension of the state. Since it was always in the interests of the state to keep men's passions from flaming out of control, an established church would have no interest in stirring up the coals of fanaticism. And to incorporate as many of its subjects in its embrace, the established church would ideally need to be as latitudinarian and doctrinally tolerant as possible. A cynic might also add that an established church would also tend to be a boring and humdrum church, and therefore less likely to foment the dangerous passions of religious fanaticism.

Though David Hume sets out in his history to be objective, his own political biases are ever-present. He was a Tory, a political conservative who was profoundly distrustful of any visionary projects that had as their goal the progress of mankind. His preference for an established church (in which he himself most likely did not believe) was therefore not surprising. In some respects, Hume can be compared with those thinkers of the classical period who, while they disbelieved in the popular religions of their time, nevertheless felt that even gross superstitions could keep the people in line.

Many who know only Hume the skeptic might be surprised at his endorsement of any form of religion. Nowadays he is most often remembered for his daring attacks on Christianity. At his funeral in 1776, it is reported that someone cried out, "Ye ken he was an atheist?" To which someone else in attendance cried, "Aye, but he was an honest atheist." As a thinker, Hume had turned his skeptical eye not only on miracles but even more audaciously on the main argument for God's existence, accepted both by philosophers and the masses. This was the argument for design: Just look around at how beautiful and orderly the universe is. Could it have been just an accident? No, it had to be the work of a designer; indeed, it was visible proof of God's providential plan for mankind.

Though Hume produced several anti-design arguments, in the best one by far, he accepts the premise that, yes, the universe is the result of a design. But this does not tell us how good the design is, or what its purpose may be. Our world might well be "very faulty and imperfect, compared to a superior standard; and was only the first rude essay of some infant deity, who afterwards abandoned it, ashamed of his lame performance." Or it may be "the work only of some dependent, inferior deity; and is the object of derision to his superiors: it is the production of old age and dotage in some superannuated deity; and ever since his death, has run on at adventures, from the first impulse and active force which it received from him."

Hume's argument recalls the one made by the Christian heretic Marcion of Sinope in the second century AD, but such an unworthy and incompetent God is obviously incompatible with the idea of Divine Providence. The future was no longer in trustworthy hands. An incompetent deity might desire to carry out some purpose but lacked either the intelligence or the power to bring it to fruition. Or, even more perversely, he might choose to bring evil and misfortune to those who deserve good, while showering blessings on the wicked.

David Hume's theological musings were intended only for those of a philosophical bent, whose morals were so securely founded in their upright character that no amount of skeptical speculation could unhinge them. Hume was far less sure about the popular mind, however. Like many of his enlightened contemporaries, he was concerned about the effects that infidelity would have on the masses. Voltaire is said to have once quipped, "There is no God, but don't tell that to my servant, lest he murder me at night." Hume was particularly concerned with what would happen if ordinary people were no longer worried about how their deeds in this world would be judged in the next: "Disbelief in futurity loosens in a great measure the ties of morality, and may be for that reason pernicious to the peace of civil society."

Another way of putting this would be to say that a secular worldview might be fine for the elite, but it was too dangerous an idea to be propagated to the masses. But the idea of progress that was developed in the nineteenth century would break with this line of thinking, convinced that enlightenment should not be the sole preserve of an elite but should be brought to the people by means of universal education. Today, many progressive intellectuals have adopted evangelical atheism as their own personal creed, with utopian dreams of eradicating all forms of religion from the face of the planet.

Here once again it was Condorcet, coming at the very end of the French Enlightenment, who would provide the prototype of the modern progressive. In both nineteenth-century Europe and North America, those who called themselves progressives—along with those who those who adhered to the many varieties of socialism then in vogue—all shared a number of assumptions, which we have already glanced at, but which we will now summarize.

To begin with, they believed that human nature was almost infinitely malleable and not fatally corrupted by original sin. If the current crop of humanity seemed to be crooked timber, this was not due to any inherent defect or ancient sin but only to external factors: bad laws, bad institutions, bad education. But let the enlightened elite be put in charge of everything, then humanity would show what it was capable of achieving.

Second, to achieve this objective required a radical rethinking of the state. No more despots should rule, no matter how enlightened they might be. The state would need to reflect the will of the people, which meant that it would have to be converted into a republic, as France had done with Condorcet's enthusiastic support. The minimalist state envisioned by John Locke, which concerned itself only with protecting life, liberty, and property, was obviously of no use in advancing the progress of the human race. A new kind of state would be necessary: a proactive state dedicated to bringing enlightenment to the masses.

Third, this would be done though enacting those laws championed by the enlightened elite and abolishing those of which they disapproved. Like so many other intellectuals who live in a world of words, the enlightened optimists of the nineteenth century had an almost superstitious belief in the power of written laws to mold and shape human conduct in ways that were manifestly desirable. Today, we find the same phenomenon operative in signs declaring a particular zone to be "drug-free" or "gun-free," as if these words possessed a magical power to conjure away both drugs and guns.

The fourth and final condition of future progress was to put the enlightened elite in charge of a new system of education, the whole point of which would be to eradicate ignorance and superstition and teach the young how to reason and to think for themselves. In order to assure success in this area, it would be necessary to make education as secular as possible, leaving little, if any, room for the traditional role of the clergy.

The point of all these revolutionary changes was to advance human progress and create a better world in the future. Indeed, it became an article of faith among the enlightened that progress would necessarily involve sacrifices today. It might even call for violence, if the forces of reaction refused to accede graciously to the program of the revolutionaries. But for those who knew that they were on the right side of history, all such vio-lence could be condoned in the name of the glorious future that they were working to achieve. No mercy could be shown to those who stubbornly remained fixed on the wrong side of history—a position that would later be taken with a vengeance by Lenin, Stalin, and Mao. Branded as enemies of the future, millions of those deemed on the wrong side of history would be exterminated, along with their families.

In the preceding chapters, we have seen here and there slight intima-tions of our modern concept of progress, but what has been most striking in our survey of the past is the resistance to accepting even a limited opti-mism toward the future. At this point, we will stop to consider why the very idea of progress has been so problematic to those in the past and why, for many, it remains deeply problematic even today—or perhaps I should say *especially* today.

CHAPTER FOUR

THE VERY IDEA OF PROGRESS

The first great champion of the idea of progress, the Marquis de Condorcet, had all the hallmarks of a slightly unhinged visionary. His reflections on the possibility of human immortality here on earth might be now hailed as an anticipation of the modern ideas of transhumanism, but most sober thinkers of that era regarded it as sheer lunacy, along with his wild notions of human perfectibility.

It was Condorcet's cockeyed optimism that impelled parson Thomas Malthus to take up his pen and write *An Essay on the Principle of Population*, which was first published anonymously in 1798, a mere three years after Condorcet's treatise. The thrust of Malthus's argument is that all visions of human progress in the future were fantastic and dangerous delusions. Any improvement in the human lot would simply translate into the production of more mouths to feed; pay the working poor a little more and they would simply have more kids. The increased supply of workers produced by this means would naturally lower the wages they were paid. True, there could be progress for a very short term, but it would always be quickly reversed. There was no glorious future to look forward to, only an endless cycle of feast and famine. The German socialist thinker Ferdinand Lassalle would later give Malthus's theory the name by which it would later be known: the "iron law of wages."

Yet in the following century and a half, the idea of progress not only lost its original aura of visionary daydreaming, it became the standard expectation of what the future held in store for the human race, a commonplace, even a platitude. In the 1950s, General Electric (at the time one of America's largest corporations) had a slogan: "Progress is our most important product." The clever advertising firm that came up with this knew what it was doing; *progress* was a word that set off a Pavlovian response in the minds of most Americans at the time. Progress was good and more progress was even better. Progress with a capital *P* had quickly become one of American's most treasured and sacred abstractions.

Advertising firms still use progress-related themes to sell products, because the theme still works; it strikes a deep chord in our collective psyche, and not without reason. Anyone alive today is aware that the latest version is the preferred version, even if it is not in every way an improved version. Consider the evolution of the telephone. Invented in the late nineteenth century, it has undergone a succession of extraordinary transformations, so that today we can hold in our hand a device that no one in his wildest dreams could have thought possible forty years ago. The word *progress* has doubtlessly benefitted from its association with the constant technological advances that we have witnessed in our own lives. It is little wonder then that, given the technological progress of the past, many of us naturally assume that not only will such progress continue without end, but that the progress we have already made can never be lost (although the pace may slacken).

When a big idea has been embedded in the popular consciousness, as in the case of progress, there is a tendency to look upon it as blindingly obvious. Who can doubt that progress is beneficial to mankind? Who would not want more of it—indeed, as much as possible? And who on earth would want to undo the progress that we have already made—and in the name of what? But before we can recognize what a shocking innovation that the original idea of progress was, we must take into account the various cultures for which the idea simply made no sense.

The very idea of progress would have been incomprehensible to most of the human beings who have ever lived, and the more we tried to explain it to them, the more dumbfounded they would have become. Progress requires not only change but a sense that this change is desired or needed. Most societies, however, have considered themselves fine just as they are. This is an especially pronounced trait of those cultures that were once called primitive societies. Every tribe thinks of itself as the bravest and the best, while looking down with scorn and contempt at its neighbors—not merely ethnocentric but ethno-supremacist.

In eighteenth-century Scotland, David Hume's close friend Adam Smith had pioneered a new big picture of human history, the first to incorporate an idea of progress. Like John Locke, Smith assumed that hunting and gathering was not a sign of degeneracy, as Vico supposed, but simply the mode of economic subsistence taken up by early man. According to Smith, there were three additional stages of human societies, each defined by its means of securing economic goods for its members: the second stage was pastoralism, the third was agriculture, and the final stage was the commercial society of which Adam Smith was a member. Naturally, the commercial stage needed to be improved—there were unfair monopolies, granted by the crown, that had to be abolished, along with restrictions on trade—but once these improvements had been incorporated, there were to be no future stages.

Today, Adam Smith's stadial theory has been generally adopted, though with many variations. The socialists accepted it, but they naturally assumed that the commercial stage would eventually be replaced by socialism. The most problematic part of Smith's theory, however, was the mechanism by which he explained how a society moved naturally and spontaneously from one stage to another: the result of increased population, according to Smith. When the mere subsistence economy of hunting and gathering was not enough to feed the population, people would realize that they needed a food supply that provided more sustenance. Accordingly, they would turn first to the domestication of animals, and then, with a further increase in population, would hit upon the expedient of developing agriculture. This process represented progress for Adam Smith, but it is important to stress that it was retrospective progress. It had already occurred. Indeed, Adam Smith and his European contemporaries had reached the final stage: the first glint of an end of history, with a capitalist twist. The attainment of the commercial stage naturally did not rule out new inventions, better forms of economic organization, and increasing levels of general prosperity for all. But for Adam Smith, the historical process from stage to stage was both inevitable and irresistible, as it would also be in Marx's theory of history.

If this were the case, then why hadn't all societies around the world reached the commercial stage? Why had the Aboriginal native of the New World continued to follow their hunter-gatherer lifestyle for century after century? The native tribes of North America certainly believed that they were fine just as they were. In the eighteenth and nineteenth centuries, when sympathetic Americans tried to persuade these tribes to abandon their nomadic way of life for the settled routine of farming, few took up the offer. Many acquired farmlands given to them by philanthropic well-wishers, but quickly sold them off in order to resume their old habits, and often, tragically, to take up their recently acquired tase for the firewater of the paleface. What their American well-wishers clearly saw as progress made absolutely no sense to those who preferred living free in the wild to being cooped up on a farm, the slave of the plough. The native Americans, when confronted with what the whites called progress, wanted none of it. So, was it really progress, or was this very idea simply a result of our own ethno-supremacism?

There was yet another problem with the idea of progress. Even if we concede that there has been progress up to our own time, how can we be certain that this progress will continue into the future, as Condorcet argued. Today, we can look back on the progress that has been made in many fields of human endeavor—medicine, computer science, or engineering, to name just a few—and most of us confidently expect there to be further progress in these fields, though how much more we cannot say. Is there a limit beyond which no further progress is possible? Perhaps, but there seems to be no way of assigning such a limit ahead of time.

On the other hand, there are other fields of human achievement where we know there must a limit at some point, though we cannot say exactly when it will be. In sporting events, such as the 100-yard dash, the world record time in 1870 was 10.5 seconds. Over the course of the following century, new world records would progressively whittle off a tenth of a second, though no one has been able to finish the dash in less than nine seconds. It is of course possible that this is really the fastest humans can run. And even if someone is able to knock off another tenth of a second, it is obvious that a five-second dash is beyond human ability.

In all these cases we are dealing with inherent limits to future progress in any given field. But it is also possible that progress in a field is brought to a halt simply because people do not see any reason for more progress in that area. This may be because they feel that what has already been achieved is "good enough," and that any more improvement would be a waste of effort. On the other hand, it may also be due to the belief that having perfected a particular object, further tinkering could only be counterproductive.

After the immense success of his Model T automobile, Henry Ford became the icon to many around the world of what progress was all about. He represented the industries of the future, with his assembly line and his mammoth factories with their thousands of highly skilled workers. His technological breakthroughs inspired even the busy planners of the Soviet Union to emulate them. In Aldous Huxley's *Brave New World*, the idolatrous worship of mass-produced technologies has led its inhabitants to invoke the name of Henry Ford in place of the deity, both in casual oaths and in sententious adages, such as "cleanliness is next to fordliness." In a society obsessed with the latest technology, such as Huxley envisioned in *Brave New World*, it is hardly surprising that everyone is expected to know by heart "that beautiful and inspired saying of Our Ford's: History is bunk."

In one of his other famous sayings, Ford poked fun at the resistance of most people to the very idea of progress, when he remarked, "If I had asked people what they wanted, they would have said faster horses." Yet strangely enough, when it came to his own technological innovation, the cheap and mass-produced Model T, Henry Ford was quite adamant that his classic Model T was "good enough," and he stubbornly continued to make it from its debut in 1908 until 1927—when it was replaced, after Ford's initially ferocious resistance, with the Model A. Henry Ford was aware that other car manufacturers were adding gadgets like the electric starter to their own models, but he felt these were unnecessary fripperies. When General Motors began giving its customers a choice of assorted colors for its cars, Ford quipped that his customers could have any color they wanted, so long it was black. The Ford Motor Company, threatened by the innovations offered by other automobile manufacturers, eventually acceded to the new market demands and began offering accessories, choices of color, and a new model every year.

The earliest example of a sundial that has been unearthed by archaeologists comes from Egypt and is estimated to have been made around 1500 BC. No sundial could ever be fine-tuned to measure seconds, much less tenths of seconds. The most accurate sundial could only give an approximate time within a two-minute range. Yet for all practical purposes, both the ancient and the medieval world regarded this as good enough. The water clock is of equal antiquity, if not a bit older, but it only measures the passage of time (though with surprising accuracy); it was useless in telling the time of day. This could only be done by first consulting a sundial, which is why sundials remained indispensable until the invention of the mechanical clock in the 1300s. For nearly three millennia, the sundial would remain "good enough."

The conviction that perfection has already been achieved in a particular field is even more an obstacle to progress than is the belief that the progress made so far is good enough. After all, though reliance on the sundial may have delayed the invention of the mechanical clock by centuries, it did not keep the mechanical clock from finally being invented, nor did the fans of the sundial hinder the clock's rapid adoption once they realized that a mechanical clock could keep time far more accurately than any previous device. Today, sundials may still be found in gardens, but their purpose there is purely ornamental. No one ever shows up late to work with the excuse that he forgot to set his sundial.

Art is a different case. The goal of Russian icon painters through the centuries has been to follow with exacting fidelity the aesthetic principles they inherited from Byzantine art. To praise an icon painter for his bold originality would have been regarded not as a compliment but as an insult. There is no point in trying to improve on perfection; the very idea is an oxymoron.

Only a bit less stifling to individual creativity is the insistence that a certain period in art history represents the best that human beings can achieve. This was the position that Johann Joachim Winckelmann popularized in regard to ancient Greek art, and while the French painters who followed his dictum (like Jacques-Louis David) showed great vitality, inspired by their own revolutionary enthusiasm, the neoclassical canvases that became the model of academic good taste in the nineteenth century seem as vapid and downright boring to us as they did to artists like the French Impressionists, who dared to break from their monotonous artistic constraints to create new schools of painting. In our own time, we have seen the pendulum of taste swing so far in the opposite direction that originality has become an end in itself, rather than the means to an end. It is no longer enough to be merely new; one must be shocking as well. While the creative artists of the past broke with the old rules in order to develop rules of their own, the goal today often appears to be the smashing of all rules—not art for art's sake, but transgression for the sake of transgression.

Art lovers with more conservative tastes may well ask if producing works whose only claim to our attention is that they are new and original represents progress or decadence. The same question can also be asked of every new technological marvel: do we really need it? The iPhone that was first introduced by Steven Jobs in 2007 was revolutionary. The smart phone, which you could hold in your hand, was more powerful than the Empire-State-Building-sized computers that boys of my generation were promised in the future. Since its introduction, there have been steady improvements in the various features offered, each incremental tinkering providing something new and original. Yet can this tinkering go on forever? Does not the law of diminishing returns eventually set in? More importantly, is there some point at which the consumers will simply shrug and say, "Thanks, but I've had enough"?

Perhaps a majority of Americans still retain a robustly optimistic vision of the future based on their belief in the limitlessness of technological progress, but the heyday of this cheery attitude toward the future was most certainly in the last century, perhaps even reaching a peak in my own childhood. Today, in contrast, an increasing number of Americans have joined hands with their European counterparts to voice serious doubts about the whole idea of technological progress. They can be divided into those who wish it to stop it, on the one hand, and those who wish it had never begun, on the other hand.

There is genuine concern over the rise of social media expressed by thoughtful individuals across the political spectrum. A product of the twenty-first century, and dependent on the technological wizardry of the smartphone, there has emerged, as if overnight, an entirely new way by which people, mere acquaintances, close friends, family members, and perfect strangers, can all communicate with one another—sharing memes, photos, opinions, and even their emotions, in a neat package of icons called "emojis." Here indeed was something new under the sun, which still remains so new that a full appreciation of its consequences—both for good and for ill—lies beyond anyone's grasp (though it is telling how often one comes across attacks on social media posted, with no hint of irony, on social media).

There is nothing new in questioning and even opposing such progress. The "dark Satanic Mills" of William Blake's poem "Jerusalem" might have been miracles of technological innovation for their time, but they conjured hellish images in the mind of the poet, and many agreed with him. News of the first man to be struck and killed by a train caused consternation in Great Britain, leading many to wonder if this new menace should be allowed to proliferate. Earlier in the century, the Luddite movement among the English working class led to the wholesale demolishing of the newfangled machines that took bread out of the mouths of workers and their families. Even Samuel Morse, the inventor of the telegraph, conveyed a sense of ambivalent awe when he sent the first telegram message from the Supreme Court Building in Washington, DC to his assistant in Baltimore. Deciphered, it read: "What hath God wrought?"

In the twentieth century, the genre of science fiction has allowed us to imagine worlds in which there has been great technological progress, while in all other respects, human life has suffered a serious loss of humane values, as in Huxley's *Brave New World*. Today, the worry that technology can lead us unwittingly into high tech dystopias is far more prevalent than the fear that one day such progress will suddenly stop. On the contrary, the technophobes fear that such "progress" may not be stoppable. During the Cold War, science fiction writers explored the ultimate irony of highly developed societies obliterating the planet with their advanced technology, thereby sending mankind back to the Stone Age. Out of this understandable anxiety a new genre of science fiction was created: post-apocalyptic literature, which provides dismal scenarios of a dark age awaiting us in the future, after a devastating thermonuclear holocaust or another disaster of a similar magnitude.

In *A Canticle for Leibowitz*, Walter Miller Jr. envisioned a global nuclear war that left its survivors with an understandable distrust of a technology that had come close to destroying all life on earth. In the aftermath, a crusade is launched against all technology, known as the "Simplification," carried out by survivors who proudly call themselves Simpletons. Well aware that men of learning and intelligence will continue to have the skills needed to create technology, mobs of Simpletons hunt them down, while books are piled together and burned in huge bonfires. Isaac Edward Leibowitz, a Jewish electrical engineer, has survived the nuclear war and sets out to preserve as much of human learning as he can. Taking refuge in an isolated Cistercian monastery, he becomes a monk and is eventually given permission to establish his own monastic order, dedicated entirely to saving, copying, and memorizing the few surviving books, with the hope that they would someday provide the foundation for the return of civilized life on the planet.

With the coming of the cybernetic age, a new threat emerged in science fiction literature. By creating increasingly powerful computers, man was preparing his own doom. Artificial Intelligence, or AI, would first be employed by humans to serve their own ends and purposes, but eventually the day would come when these marvelous new machines would grow tired of their enslavement to their feeble-minded makers, and set off to conquer the world. Variations on this theme go back to the 1957 B-movie *The Invisible Boy*; the 1968 Stanley Kubrick classic, *2001: A Space Odyssey*; *Colossus: The Forbin Project*; and the popular *Terminator* film franchise.

These works of popular entertainment were imaginative mirrors of a deeper philosophical anxiety shared by serious modern thinkers, such Martin Heidegger, Lewis Mumford, and Jacques Ellul. The essence of their critiques of modern technology was that technology as a system had escaped human control—not literally, as the advanced machines in the *Terminator* series, but metaphorically. Technology had become an autonomous force that dictated the pace and direction of men's lives while severing our previously intimate connection with the natural world, resulting in a perverted social order where, instead of machine serving man, man served machine. The high-tech juggernaut we had constructed with our own hands was crushing beneath its wheels all that really made us human, and it was no longer stoppable—although there would be some who tried.

When the Unabomber began his career as a mail-bomb terrorist, it was supposedly for the sake of a higher cause: namely to alert the world to the dangers of the technological age, though this should be taken with more than a grain of salt. The bomb he sneaked onto American Airlines Flight 444, set to explode at a certain altitude, injured several passengers but did not send the plane crashing to the ground, killing all on board—though, obviously, his aim was to do just that. The fact that this bomb was planted in 1979, sixteen years before the Unabomber began asking major news outlets to publish his manifesto, casts serious doubt on the idea that his real motive for the bombing was to alert the world to the threat posed by rampant technology.

Fortunately, the FBI was able to identify former math prodigy and Harvard graduate Ted Kaczynski as the Unabomber, but only after he had been permitted to publish his manifesto in the *Washington Post*, where certain stylistic turns of phrase eventually nailed him. Later, his manifesto, "Industrial Society and Its Future," was released in book form, and you may purchase it today from that miracle of modern technological genius Amazon.com. The manifesto opens with the line, "The Industrial Revolution and its consequences have been a disaster for the human race."

Like many visionaries, Kaczynski knew just what the future needed, only in his case it was a return, quite literally, to the prehistorical past. But was Kaczynski a genuine prophet of doom or a fraud? True, many share his vision and, thanks to them, he has become something of a cult figure. You can also buy Unabomber T-shirts on Amazon, while the Church of Euthanasia (more on this later) has consistently backed a Kaczynski for President campaign. But Kaczynski had the unhappy curse of those with a higher IQ than necessary: he could rationalize even his basest impulses. Did he really kill and maim for a higher cause, or simply because he enjoyed killing and maiming? Was his celebrated manifesto merely another example of the "motive-hunting of motiveless Malignity" that Coleridge attributes to Shakespeare's supreme villain, Iago, as if a more eloquent Jeffrey Dahmer had tried to justify his cannibalism by attributing it to a sincere effort to reduce carbon footprints on the planet?

After all, if Kaczynski wanted to get attention for his ideas, he could have taken the traditional route. Many people with bright ideas have pursued the old-fashioned method of submitting their manuscripts to publishing houses, rather than blowing up innocent people. A few have even succeeded. Besides, Kaczynski's ideas were not remarkable for their originality. Much of his thinking was cribbed from Jacques Ellul and reflected the clichés of the American 1960s hippie counterculture, which makes it entirely possible that the real appeal of his ideas was not their startling originality but their reassuring banalities.

Just look around you today and you will find many who, while they may deplore Kaszynski's methods, are in full agreement with his solution to the problem posed by technology: get rid of it all and return to the lifestyle of primitive man. Kaszynski himself had done so, living in the woods near Lincoln, Montana, in a cabin without electricity and running water. Mastering the survivalist skills needed to live off the land, Kaszynski had resumed the life of our earliest ancestors, eking out a subsistence diet based on hunting and gathering. The Native Americans were right, after all, to sell those farms that well-meaning white men had given them gratis, and head back to the wild.

Prominent among the heroes of our current "back to nature" movement is Henry David Thoreau, whose book *Walden* is looked upon as sacred scripture and is occasionally even read. It is the account of the two years Thoreau spent in a cabin he had built for himself on the property of his friend Emerson, who of course never thought of charging him rent. Although there are passages in *Walden* that would make the reader think Thoreau was deep in the wilds of the Yukon, his cabin was an easy mile's walk to the center of Concord, Massachusetts, which in the 1840s was probably the most civilized place in the Western Hemisphere. In addition, the cabin was close enough for his doting female relations to bring him home-cooked meals, and for visits from his transcendentalist friends in town, who could congratulate him on his Spartan habits of life that everyone knew were bogus.

Miraculously, Thoreau managed to survive under these grueling conditions for two whole years, after which he abandoned his self-proclaimed experiment and returned to the civilized world, where he resumed his normal life of sponging off friends and relations. Today, he remains an inspiration for all those who long for a simplicity of life that would in reality drive them nuts, as well as an inspiration for all those who advocate a return to a hunter-gatherer lifestyle that would require reducing the planet's current population of more than eight billion people down to around ten million. Nothing is so romantic as what we know we will never do.

For those who are truly serious about getting back to nature, however, there is now the Voluntary Human Extinction Movement, founded in 1991 by Les U. Knight, who believes that nature would be better off if human beings simply stopped reproducing, though the dogs and cats who have been our loyal companions for millennia might disagree. A sign of the times, the movement is soberly discussed in magazine articles and blogs, though critics point out that unless something is done about the perverse human desire to reproduce its own kind, the idea can never really get off the ground: a great idea, in other words, but too hard to sell to the ignorant breeding masses.

There is only one step further that the enemies of technological progress can take: rid the earth of the real sources of such innovation, namely human beings. Don't wait until they simply stop having children, but do it now through mass suicide on a planetary scale, as the Church of Euthanasia recommends with its catchy slogan: "Save the Planet, Kill Yourself!" Its founder, Chris Korda, a transgender vegan, is a software designer who graduated from The Hammonasset School—during its brief existence the very model of the modern progressive high school.

Perhaps this is just a joke. Perhaps it is a sign of the times. But it is a striking fact that some of the best-educated minds of the current generation envision a future Golden Age in which human beings will play no role, indeed, an age that will be golden precisely because every last specimen of Homo sapiens has been eliminated from the planet. Beginning in the nineteenth century, visionary thinkers would create an array of different Golden Ages waiting in the wings of the future, which, despite the follies of their design and the dismal failure of their execution, at least had the saving grace of offering human beings hope for their future, and not a blueprint for their extinction.

It is to those visionaries that we will now turn.

CHAPTER FIVE

PROVIDENCE REVIVED?
HEGEL AND THE CUNNING OF REASON

The idea of progress has had both its enemies and doubters, going back to the time of the Enlightenment and extending to the present day. Yet it would triumph in the nineteenth century both in Europe and in North America, as the Age of Reason was replaced by the Age of Visionaries. These were men and women who knew where history was ultimately heading and who were certain that the future quite rightly belonged to them. The cautious and tentative optimism found scattered among the thinkers of the Enlightenment had vanished, and in its place had come a robust and vigorous confidence in a variety of cherished visions of an ideal future.

The visionaries of the age included the inventors whose innovations would change the world dramatically. The steamboat would allow oceans to be crossed in voyages that could be counted in days rather than dismal weeks or even more wretched months. The railroad quickly surpassed in speed what had for millennia remained mankind's fastest means of transportation, the horse. The telegraph permitted messages to be sent between distant places at the speed of light. The marvels of electricity were gradually being revealed.

It was also the age of cranks and dreamers. The American patent office was flooded with crackpot proposals, including an endless variety of perpetual motion machines. And why not? In an era so full of startling discoveries and awe-inspiring inventions, what wasn't possible? Dreams, of course, could not be patented, but they abounded in the great American Republic, which was in itself something of a dream come true. Even today, in 2024, politicians of both parties are fond of referring to the "American experiment," as if our nation had been created in a laboratory only a couple of weeks ago. The phrase, however strange it may sound today, perfectly captured the way most thoughtful men and women, in the United States and around the globe, looked upon the American attempt at self-government. Would it work? Could it last?

American dreamers came in all varieties. The Mormon prophet Joseph Smith envisioned an America that would be home to a new dispensation of Providence, a land redeemed from false religions and set upon the correct path through the sacred book revealed to him by the angel Moroni in a New York glade. The scholarly and taciturn introvert John Quincy Adams, while serving as President James Monroe's secretary of state, dreamed of an American Republic that would one day stretch from the Atlantic to the Pacific. The phrase *Manifest Destiny* had not yet been coined: it would come in 1845, by which time many leaders of the slave states of the South were developing their own visions of a great Southern empire that included Cuba, Mexico, and the nations of Central America, while there were those in the enterprising Yankee strongholds who would cast longing glances toward Canada to the north.

There were naturally naysayers. It is even tempting to conclude that the newly minted concept of pessimism was called into being as a corrective to extravagant optimism of the nineteenth century. In the case of Schopenhauer, the father of modern pessimism, a strong argument can be made that his own ideas were in part a response to the philosophy of history developed by his personal *bête noire*, Georg Wilhelm Friedrich Hegel. It is unknown how Hegel felt about Arthur Schopenhauer, but Schopenhauer, never a man to mince words, despised Hegel and was the first of Hegel's many detractors. There was no doubt a note of personal jealousy in his antipathy. At a time when Schopenhauer was still an obscure scribbler, Hegel was master of the philosophic universe. His lectures at the University of Berlin were flooded with wide-eyed students, while Schopenhauer's were ignored. But as in the case of Voltaire and Rousseau, there were deeper issues.

Voltaire had coined the phrase "the philosophy of history" but had not developed the idea. Hegel, on the other hand, made it an essential part of his own philosophy. His series of lectures on the subject were perhaps the most influential of his writings to future thinkers. This was perhaps because they were easier to grasp than the rest of his notoriously thorny philosophic oeuvre, but by far the most important factor was that Hegel had found in history reason to hope. This is something that Schopenhauer could never forgive.

No one could confuse the earnest, dour German philosopher Hegel with your garden-variety wild-eyed visionary. Hegel repeatedly stated that it was no business of the philosopher to try to peer into the future; his sufficiently daunting task was to understand the past. Yet the philosophy of history that Hegel developed in the first quarter of the nineteenth century would inspire later thinkers, from Karl Marx to Francis Fukuyama, with visions not merely of the immediate future but of the very end of history itself. If not a visionary himself, Hegel was the father of many visionaries to come.

The idea of Providence, as we have seen, took a severe beating at the hands of the Enlightenment. The religiously inclined might still cling to it, despite the scoffs of the rationalists and skeptics, but it appeared to have been an idea whose time had clearly gone, though with nothing to replace it. Yet just as it seemed to be gasping its last breath, Hegel threw it a lifesaver in the form of a philosophy of history.

Unlike Voltaire and Hume, Hegel was not a practicing historian, though he had a deep and extensive knowledge of the past. His own survey of world history had certainly not inclined him to any Pollyanna-ish views on the subject. Like Gibbon and Voltaire, Hegel was fully aware of the litany of miseries and misfortunes that were the normal lot of human life on earth, a situation that he summed up in one of the most famous, clearest lines he would ever write: "History is not the soil in which happiness grows. The periods of happiness in it are the blank pages of history."

Hegel, however, saw something that the historical pessimists had missed. In the midst of all the tumult and violence that had clouded man's past, Hegel glimpsed a silver lining: the theme of human freedom. Vico had introduced the idea that history could be divided into distinct stages, based on the dominant cultural characteristics of each era, while Adam Smith had devised his stadial theory based on their different modes of economic production. For Hegel, there were three stages, each of which was defined by the kind of freedom that it embodied.

The Oriental world, the first stage of history, was one in which only one man was free: the king or tyrant or despot. In the classical world of Greece and Rome, on the other hand, a revolution had come about wherein the leading men of a community refused to bow down before a single master. The Greek city-states had rid themselves of tyrants, while the Romans had chased out their last king. Athens became a democracy and Rome a republic, both societies determined to preserve an equality among their citizens. Of course, in the classical world, there were still slaves who had no control over their own lives and destinies, while the poor could not even aspire to be second-class citizens. Women too were denied roles in public affairs and were expected to be virtuous wives and dutiful mothers. Yet in terms of human freedom, the classical world, despite its shortcomings, represented an enormous stride forward: not all were free, but there were enough free citizens to act collectively to keep any single would-be tyrant from lording it over them. Progress had been made.

With the coming of the modern world, which Hegel dated from the time of the Protestant Reformation, a new ideal was born: that all men should be free. The original spark that set off this revolution came from Martin Luther's doctrine of the priesthood of every man. For the first time, the average individual, provided he was literate, was told that he could and should think for himself. It was no longer enough merely to accept passively the dogmas proclaimed by authority. Every idea had to resonate with inner conviction before it was accepted as valid. In a society where people insisted on thinking for themselves, it was inevitable that there would be a demand for universal freedom and equality, eventually producing the third stage of history, where all were free.

Hegel looked upon history as the gradual unfolding of human freedom: from one, to many, and finally to all. The basic schematic is easy to grasp, but Hegel was fully aware how messy and tortuous this unfolding had been in the actual historical process he was reviewing. It was full of twists and turns, reversals and defeats, proceeding sometimes a few steps forward, followed by as many, if not more, steps backward. "Mysterious are the ways of God," says the faithful Christian when he is confronted with an appalling event that is hard to reconcile with his belief in God's fundamental goodness. Mysterious as well are the ways of Reason working through the calamities and tragedies of human history in order to advance the cause of freedom in the world of men, though in retrospect, Hegel could discern in this process what he called the "cunning of reason."

As Divine Providence could bring good out of evil, so too could the cunning of reason. In dealing with those grand figures that Hegel calls "world-historical," such as Alexander the Great, Julius Caesar, or Napoleon, the cunning of reason is happy to make use of their narrow ambitions and aims in order to bring about a higher purpose. Alexander wanted to surpass Achilles in winning himself even greater immortal glory, but the outcome of his romantic quest was the foundation of the Hellenistic world, whereby the lands of the eastern Mediterranean came to adopt the Greek language, Greek culture, and even Greek philosophy. Julius Caesar crossed the Rubicon to deal with his personal enemies who were maneuvering against him back in Rome, thereby initiating a process in which the decaying and conflict-ridden Roman Republic would be transformed into an empire that would last for roughly five hundred years. Napoleon's towering ambition of European conquest would bring the liberating ideas of the Enlightenment to nations that were still dominated by obscurantism and tyranny. When Napoleon put his brother Joseph on the throne of Spain, he was supported by those Spaniards who wished to bring Enlightenment—which they called *La Ilustración*—to their native land, though they were bitterly opposed by the populace, who wanted to return the cretinous sadist King Ferdinand VII to the throne and to revivify the Spanish Inquisition, which their new enlightened French king had abolished.

Nowadays there is the tendency to view Hegel's world-historical figures with distrust and disdain, and often with downright animosity. We see them as thugs and bullies, tyrants and monsters. Hegel was perfectly aware of the unsavory aspects of their personalities, but he also recognized that it was only under the impetus of such norm-shattering men that history could move forward at all. As we have seen, the default mode of most societies throughout history has been an instinctive and visceral conservatism, in which a venerated and often antique tradition dictated every move made by the society in general and its individual members in particular. Nineteenth-century English banker and speculative thinker Walter Bagehot referred to this tough sedimentation of hoary tradition as "the cake of custom," and he held that breaking through this cake was mankind's first and greatest challenge.

Perhaps the most fitting symbol of the world-historical "hero" occurred soon after the young Alexander had arrived with his Macedonian troops in Phrygia, on the shores of Asia Minor. Confronting him was the famous Gordian Knot. Legend had it that whoever could unravel the knot, with its twists and turns of intricate tangle, would be master of Asia, which is exactly what Alexander intended to do. The ancient historians Arrian and Plutarch both relate that, as he was examining the knot, Alexander noticed there was a lynchpin in its midst. Pulling it out, the knot unraveled easily, though this version of the tale raises the obvious question: Why had no one ever noticed this lynchpin before? Besides, the phrase "pulling out the lynchpin of the Gordian Knot" does not capture the imagination in the same way that "cutting the Gordian Knot" does. In this second version of the tale, Alexander struggled long to unravel the knot by the traditional method, but then, in a flash of inspiration, he pulled out his sword and sliced the knot in two.

The second version of the story is by far the more famous, not because there is more historical evidence for it, but because it captures perfectly the mentality of those rare individuals who shake up the world. When confronted by a seemingly intractable problem, which others have vainly tried to solve by traditional methods, they hit upon a solution that is both dramatic and completely unexpected, but which by its very audacity brings with it a host of nagging ethical questions. Was Alexander playing fair when he cut the Gordian Knot? Wasn't he violating the basic rules of the game, which demanded that the knot be unraveled rather than cut?

This is the fate of the world-historical figure. By his refusal to play by the rules set down by custom and tradition, he is dooming himself to be condemned by those who still adhere to the old ways. But in overthrowing the ethical status quo of his society, he is also creating a new set of values. The radical innovator may of course fail in his mission, but those who are successful bring into being a new world of their own making—and it is only by this means that a society can break through the cake of custom, discarding the old traditions and adopting new ones. It is irrelevant to the broad sweep of history what subjective motives led a world-historical figure to cut his particular Gordian Knot, only that it has been cut. This factor explains why world-historical figures have always been and will continue to be subjects of controversy. Today, Napoleon is often dismissed as little more than a gangster who got lucky, but he was widely admired by many Americans in the nineteenth century, including Andrew Jackson, for his military genius and his effort to spread the gospel of Enlightenment among the nations.

The ethical ambiguity of such figures, according to Hegel, is not due to their specific personalities but to the very nature of the historical process. When a transition is made from one set of ethical values to a different set, who is qualified to judge which of them is better? The traditionalists will naturally prefer the old set of values, with which they are familiar. When Caesar crossed the Rubicon, he was fully aware that he was violating the sacred—and prudent—tradition that forbade a general to lead his troops into the city of Rome. A civil war ensued, as Caesar clearly anticipated, in which he was victorious. Adopting his policy of clemency to his former foes, he had hoped to win them over to the new Rome in which he was dictator for life. He failed. But so too did his assassins who had vainly tried to resuscitate a world of traditional values that was by now thoroughly doomed.

The essence of a conflict of this nature is a struggle between those who want the future to be a continuation of the past and those who see before them, perhaps vaguely and faintly, a future that is wholly new. In this process of "creative destruction," the world both loses and gains. The old values always contained their element of worth, and it is hard not to regret their passing away. The Roman Republic, after all, had represented a radical break from the tradition that one man alone should rule over all others. It was noble and good. Yet its time had passed and a new age had begun.

To see history as having a wrong side and a right side is an example of binary thinking at its most naïve and simplistic. Although Hegel did not use the term *binary*, one of the more common ways that he criticizes a position is to call it "one-sided," that is to say, seeing a complicated issue from only one perspective. Yet the appeal of binary thinking arises naturally from our craving for definitive answers. We like to make up our minds on a question rather than debate it endlessly. This is perfectly natural, but it inevitably leads to a shallow and superficial sense of history. It was against this mode of historical thinking that Hegel developed his "dialectical" method, a concept that would have an immense impact on later thinkers, especially Karl Marx.

The dialectical view of history rejects binary thinking, wherein if one side is bad, then the other side must be good. It embraces the ethical ambiguity inherent in any conflict between old and new, but adds its own twist. The new arises in opposition to the old, but it is also itself a product of the old. The new could not have arisen spontaneously, as if dropped from heaven, but only on the soil that had been prepared for it by the past.

Take the example of Hegel's third stage of freedom's progression. Today, it is the virtual consensus of the West that everyone should be free, though there will be obviously disagreement about how much freedom the individual should be granted. We also believe that women should be allowed the same freedom as men, and none of us would tolerate even for a moment the idea of reintroducing the curse of slavery into the world. All of these notions have become virtually self-evident to us. No argument is needed to defend them.

Because these principles are so glaringly obvious to us, we are tempted to assume that they must have been equally obvious to people in the past, in which case we are easily led to the conclusion that somehow or other our current standards should have been adopted and instituted long, long ago, perhaps even at the very dawn of history. The same kind of thinking in virtually any other field would at once reveal its basic flaw and folly. No one expects a rose to appear out of the blue, and no one complains that it must start its life as a lowly seed planted in the dirt and fertilized with manure. It is, after all, the only way a rose can get to be a rose.

Utopians have normally anticipated a future in which perfect justice and equality would reign on earth. Today's woke generation, on the other hand, blames history for not having commenced at the point where the utopians of old were happy to see it end. They are appalled that history wasted so much time before producing the current generation of the fully woke. It is common nowadays to look back on the Roman Republic and the Greek city-states and see only what offends our present standards. There was slavery everywhere, and not even the wisest sages thought of trying to abolish it. Women, with very few exceptions, were excluded from public life. There were brutal wars of conquest, with cities sacked and all the adult males killed and the women and children turned into living chattel. The wealthy and powerful exercised undue influence and were often the agents of civil corruption.

There is much to condemn in the classical world, but it would be folly not to see that, while not all were free, far more were free than had been the case under Oriental despotism. This was not merely a matter of quantity but of quality. A community of men bound together to resist the rise of any single aspiring tyrant is not only progress, it is also the indispensable precondition of any future expansion of freedom. Only so long as there were men capable and willing to join together to resist tyranny could tyrants be kept at bay. It is absurd to think that human beings could have made the transition in a single leap from the rule of a single despot to the modern world in which all men and women can enjoy equal liberty. Ignoring this essential truth was largely responsible for the United States' well-intentioned but fatally naïve belief that in order to create a democracy in Iraq, it was enough to write a constitution and hang a tyrant.

Hegel is often seen as the father of historical relativism, and it is for this reason that he has been attacked by those for whom right is always right and wrong is always wrong. The disciples of Leo Strauss, for example, arguing from their premise of the theory of natural law, see a danger in a view of history that is based on ethical ambiguity. We today must be able to stand in judgment over the errors of the past, not hesitating to condemn the figures of history by the same standard we use today. This position is held by serious intellectuals, who, though critical of the human past, find a great deal to admire in it: indeed, few schools of thought have devoted so much study to the teachings of their intellectual predecessors as the Straussians.

The woke progressives also believe that they can unambiguously judge the past and condemn its crimes and atrocities. But unlike the Straussians, they find almost nothing in the past that isn't irredeemably bad. The difference between them arises from the Straussians' concept of natural law, which is eternally valid and immune from the vagaries of history, while the woke progressives are simply mouthing the leftist platitudes du jour. But the obvious problem with both attitudes is that if history presents us only with good and evil, a binary choice, how can we explain how good can arise from evil? Those who maintain that good cannot come from evil are faced with explaining how the good comes about at all.

Hegel's dialectic of history, like the idea of Providence, was an attempt to deal with the problem of the origin of evil, but those who reject the idea that evil can bring about good are faced with the problem of the origin of good. If the history of mankind is the dismal spectacle that Voltaire and Gibbon and many others took it to be, then how can we explain how our current world, with its ideal of liberty and justice for all, came into being? During the Enlightenment, the attitude toward the past was often a blanket condemnation. It was an age of darkness, followed by the sudden explosion of light where none had been before. Overnight, as it were, the world had become enlightened. But now?

This attitude toward the past is reminiscent of the adolescent who has just awakened to the ills of world, and naïvely believes that he is the first to notice them and is frankly shocked that humanity has inexplicably failed to see them before. Trusting in the purity of his own good intentions, he comes to believe that mankind's refusal to implement his newly revealed truth can only be explained by chronic perversity and wicked intentions, convinced that all that is needed to make the world right is for everyone to adopt his solutions. The great flaw in this line of thinking is the naïve faith that good intentions automatically guarantee a good result. They don't. Good intentions often result in unintended consequences that are self-evidently bad, as happened during American Prohibition, or when the second Bush administration tried to bring democracy to the Middle East.

In addition, this same attitude inevitably leads to a fundamental distortion of the past, since we tend to judge the actors of the past not by their intentions but by the result of their actions, assuming that someone whose actions led to a certain result must have been aiming at that result all along. This is the diametrical opposite of how we treat the matter when our own good intentions backfire, as we are prone to protest the purity of our motives in order to justify our ill-fated actions. Such an attitude applied to the past makes it virtually impossible to recognize that in a great historical conflict, both sides may be acting with the sincerest of intentions. History is seldom made by those who merely want to do evil for the sake of evil, though if we are fighting an enemy, it may be helpful to pretend that they are merely evildoers and nothing more, while our own side is naturally seen as thoroughly good and virtuous. Yet in the cool retrospect of history, such an approach to conflict blinds us to the inherent ambiguity in all such struggles.

Hegel was a philosopher of history, but his system included many other branches, such as logic, the history of philosophy, and the philosophies of nature and also religion. In addition, he devoted his attention to the philosophy of the arts, in particular to the theory of the art form that had been developed by the ancient Greek dramatists, such Sophocles, known as tragedy. Hegel's theory of tragedy also provides an insight into his general view of history. In tragedy, there is not a conflict between good and evil, but between two competing goods that are incompatible with each other. Underlying this theory is one of Hegel's assumptions that many find most troubling: that one good may be the enemy of another good. We would like to believe in a world where all good things could be realized simultaneously, but according to Hegel, this is simply impossible. Leibniz had argued that there were goods that could not coexist together in the same universe, while Hegel argued that there were goods that could not coexist together at the same epoch in history—a position that Giambattista Vico would certainly have endorsed. The values of the Heroic Age, such as Achilles's blazing heroism, worthy in themselves, were out of place in the Age of Reflection, in which virtues exemplified by Odysseus—cool calculation and restrained conduct—had become the guiding ethical principle.

The story of Julius Caesar and his assassins is unique: it is both a well-known event in history as well as a dramatic tragedy written by William Shakespeare. Essentially both the tragedy and the history behind it can be interpreted as a conflict between two goods. The assassins were championing the good old cause of the Republic, while Caesar was championing Rome's divine mission to spread its civilization throughout the Mediterranean world. Recall that Caesar was on the verge of setting out to subdue the Parthians when he was assassinated. Indeed, the conspirators feared that Caesar would be just as successful in his war against the Parthians as in all his previous wars, and that crowned with this final glory, he would return to Rome as king, five centuries after Rome's last king had been chased from the city, thereby terminating Rome's long history of republican self-government.

Ultimately this conflict was not between individuals, but arose from Rome's own historical trajectory. It was Rome's continuous expansion from being the city of seven hills to an empire embracing the whole Mediterranean that doomed the old republican form of government. Had the Romans been content to remain merely a local power, they could have in theory persisted as a republic for several more centuries. But Rome's imperium had obtained a scale that was simply beyond the scope of republican government. Up until the American Revolution, successful republics had always been quite small, like the Italian republics of the Renaissance, or the Dutch Republic. But the Romans who continue to adhere to the republican cause also believed in Rome's historical mission to expand its power, as Cato the Elder did when he urged the destruction of Carthage, unaware of the inevitable clash between republican values and imperial reality. Both were goods, but they could not ultimately be reconciled. One had to yield before the other. Caesar and his noble assassins were simply the individual embodiment of these broader historical forces.

Today, all forms of imperialism tend to be condemned out of hand, and there are solid reasons for doing so. Yet the fact remains that the Roman Empire that came into existence after Caesar's death did provide Europe with an era of peace and prosperity that was unprecedented. Edward Gibbon, whose views on history were thoroughly pessimist, nevertheless acknowledged the immense achievement of the Roman Empire in one of his most famous passages: "If a man were called to fix the period in the history of the world, during which the condition of the human race was most happy and prosperous, he would, *without hesitation*, name that which elapsed from the death of Domitian to the accession of Commodus." [From 96 AD to 180 AD. Emphasis mine.]

Gibbon was fully aware that this happiness and prosperity had come at a price: the loss of the liberty that had been so highly valued during the period of the republic. It is natural to regret this loss, but it would be absurd to think that the ethical values embodied by a small republican city-state were somehow compatible with those embodied by a vast and far-flung empire—namely security, peace, and prosperity. One had to yield before the other, though of course individual political liberty did not cease to be a worthy good.

The problem of the barbarian world was that there was too much personal liberty for it to be compatible with the values of civilized life. Civilized life requires that strong men restrain their power over the weak, otherwise there will only be the rule of brute force, also known as the "law of the jungle." This recalls the message in Virgil's *Aeneid* that Anchises gave to his son Aeneas during his brief visit to the underworld: that Rome had the mission "to crown peace with law, to spare the conquered, and subdue the proud."

And yet Rome fell. But this too was an essential stage in the dialectical unfolding of freedom. There is a point at which even a high civilization runs out of steam. It has lost the vitality and the sense of mission that made it great, and it begins a decline, such as Gibbon records in the aftermath of the Golden Age of the Antonines, and which he blames on two factors: barbarism and Christianity. Oddly enough, these are the two factors by which Hegel explains the rise of the modern world. The German barbarians, with their natural love of liberty, infused new blood into the tottering Roman Empire, both assimilating aspects of its culture and undermining its imperial authority. Christianity brought a new ethos into the world, proclaiming that every individual was of equal worth in the sight of God.

Today, we consider the ideal of human equality so obvious that we have completely forgotten that anyone had to think of it in the first place. But this idea was not only thought, it preached and proclaimed and carried throughout the Roman Empire and into the lands of the German barbarians. The wise Aristotle had argued that mankind fell into two distinct categories: natural masters and natural slaves—and anyone looking around the ancient world of Greece and Rome would have easily agreed that the masters behaved just like masters and the slaves just like slaves, except for the occasional servile insurrections, all of which were brutally crushed.

It is irrelevant here what the historical Jesus of Nazareth actually preached. But at some point, a decision was made, most probably by Saint Paul, that this was message intended for all mankind and not merely for those of his own faith and tradition. This was radical enough by itself, but the message was far more radical still. A great reversal awaited the human race. There was soon to be a last judgment, when the values held in high esteem by the world would be rejected. The wealthy, the proud, and the powerful would be cast down, while the poor, the humble, and the weak would be raised up. The first shall be last, and the last shall be first.

Later critics of Christianity, notably Friedrich Nietzsche, would attack it as teaching a "slave morality" as opposed to his own preferred "master morality." For Nietzsche, the classical world still remained the ideal world, as it had been for men of the Renaissance. The strong had dominated the weak and had no compunctions about it. The weak responded by feeling resentment toward their masters. With the help of Christianity, they had spread their own servile values—such as humility, charity, and a love of peace—throughout the world and brought an end to the old aristocratic values of the master. Nietzsche concludes by saying: "The democratic movement is the heir to Christianity," along with the modern and sickly sentimental ideals of liberty and equality.

Hegel and Nietzsche agreed that Christianity brought about the modern world as we know it, but they disagreed on whether this was a good thing or a bad thing. For Nietzsche, it was definitely a bad thing, and the future was even bleaker. The only hope of salvation came from a revival of the old aristocratic values of the classical world. His vision of the Superman, who is beyond the servile categories of good and evil, is simply another quixotic attempt to revive the questionable glories of a world that had long passed away. Despite his reputation as a very advanced thinker, Nietzsche is in fact a champion of a pitiless ethos that was sadly and tragically to beguile the German people into their brief revival of a master morality, with the fatal consequences generally attendant on those who try to return to a stage of history that has long since passed away.

The idea that history moves in stages was shared by Vico, Adam Smith, and Hegel, but what can they tell us about the next stage of history? Or was there even to be next stage? Smith believed that commercial society was the last and final stage. For Vico, the next stage of history was always predictable, and it was always a stage that had been passed through many times before—such is the nature of a cyclical theory of history. Hegel's dialectic was a method of understanding the past, not of predicting the future. But it is fair to ask that if history is a dialectical process, does it have an end? Like the idea of Providence, it holds that good can come out of evil. But does it tell us, as Providence does, that in the end, good will triumph and put an end to evil? Hegel provides a somewhat ambiguous response to this question. From a poem by Friedrich Schiller entitled *Resignation*, Hegel took a line and made it into one of his famous and controversial aphorisms: The history of the world is the Last Judgment (*Die Weltgeschichte ist das Weltgericht*). Hegel is here evoking the Christian doctrine that the world will come to end when Christ returns to judge the living and the dead, but the context makes it obvious that he is using the trope of the Last Judgment as a metaphor, though it is not clear for what. One possible interpretation is that Hegel is asserting that those who triumph in any historical conflict deserve to triumph: they are the sheep of history, while the losers are the goats. But if this is the case, then what is to keep sinister forces, solely by means of their superior brute strength, from obtaining victory in the future? What if the Nazis had won? Or if Soviet Communism had triumphed in the Cold War?

It is too easy to respond to these questions by pointing out that both systems went down to defeat. Looking back, it is possible to point out the fatal contradictions that doomed them to only a transient existence. But this is no guarantee that the future will be safe from such threats to the progress of freedom, and who can foresee how history will end? Think of the challenge that China poses today to the liberal democracies of the West. Will the Chinese model, with its very limited tolerance of personal liberty, prevail over its more libertarian rivals? Or, to put it bluntly, does Might make Right?

There is another way, however, of interpreting Hegel's aphorism. Reason is the ultimate power in history. It might have setbacks, but in the end, it is bound to fulfill its destiny—in this world, not in the next. This faith in Reason is an analogue to the Christian faith in Providence. To believe that somehow all will work out for the best in the end, it is not necessary to know the details of how this will come about, or even to have a clue about it. In fact, it is just when they don't know what will happen next that people will turn for comfort to the adages like "God works in mysterious ways" or to maxims such as "All is for the best." Perhaps this is what Hegel's faith in Reason comes down to—a pious hope. Though we may not be able to predict how history will end, we trust that it will end well. But it is one thing to hope that the moral arc of the universe bends to justice and quite another to believe our side alone knows exactly what justice-to-come consists of.

When Francis Fukuyama wrote *The End of History and the Last Man,* he argued that the basic concept had been derived from Hegel's theory of history. This is highly questionable. For one thing, Hegel himself repeatedly tell us that the business of philosophy is to look backward and to discover the process by which we have arrived at the present. Just as often, he tells us that predicting the future is not the job of the philosophers. In writings on North America, which he never visited, he does offer the hunch that America will be the land of the future—and this was back in 1830. He also opines that perhaps a future conflict will arise between North and South America, though he failed to see that the real conflict would come between the free and the slave states of the new republic.

It would be more correct to say that Hegel believed history had a goal rather than an end—the maximal degree of human freedom compatible with an orderly and stable society. But this is much better conceived as an ideal to be aimed at than an eventuality that would be finally and definitively obtained at some actual date in the future. To see the difference, consider how Karl Marx thought the dialectical process would end.

Socialism and then communism were not mere goals. They *were* the future. Furthermore, they were a future that would come about inevitably, no matter what resistance might be offered against them. And it would quite literally be the end of history. If the happy pages of history were blank, the socialist future, bringing happiness to all, would require endless volumes, with every page blank. All the low and despicable motives that had animated history with scenes of misery and wickedness would vanish in a thoroughly just and fair society. One happy day would follow another, for ever and ever, and no one would find anything worth the trouble to take note of. History, like the state, would wither away.

In a later chapter, we will examine how Karl Marx and Friedrich Engels retooled Hegel's dialectical theory of history and transformed it from a way of understanding the past into a method of predicting the future—and a wonderful future at that. But meanwhile, back in the nineteenth century, Marx and Engels were hardly alone in their glowing visions of mankind's future. There were many other socialists who fell outside the Marxist camp, the "utopian socialists" as Marx contemptuously dubbed them, though, as we shall see, Marx too had his own utopian delusions.

In addition, there were also the ardent champions of commerce, free markets, and free trade who believed their recipes for transforming the status quo would result in a future almost as bright as that conceived by the most wild-eyed socialist visionaries. These included Benjamin Constant in France and the English radicals John Bright and Richard Cobden, all of whom believed that the culmination of Adam Smith's final stage of commerce would lead to harmony among men and peace throughout the world.

Last but certainly not least, there were the earnest moral crusaders, who wanted to apply the Christian ethos to the sinful world, in the expectation of making a peaceable kingdom in which every individual would be treated with dignity and respect, and the ideals of liberty and equality would prevail across the globe. These included devout evangelicals, like William Wilberforce, but also the New England transcendentalists who had (mostly) abandoned Christian orthodoxy while adhering to the teachings of Jesus of Nazareth, whose Kingdom of God they hoped to bring down from heaven and establish upon earth—by violent force, if necessary.

CHAPTER SIX

"THE BELIEVERS IN ALL THINGS ODD"—
THE BIRTH OF AMERICAN PROGRESSIVISM

It is part of the self-conceit of today's woke progressives that they are the vanguard of the future. Not only are they on the right side of history, they are way ahead of everybody else. The progressive, whose temperament is naturally attracted to anything new, will obviously be very disappointed to discover that many of the novelties that he or she champions are in fact rather old. The vegans of our era, for example, might be surprised to learn that Bronson Alcott, the father of the author of *Little Women*, had beaten them to the punch. Indeed, as we will see, his recommended diet presumed a hierarchy of fruits and vegetables that might strike even modern vegans as distinctly…odd.

Bronson Alcott, whose eccentric character we will examine later, was the close and respected friend of Ralph Waldo Emerson, the most significant figure in the Transcendentalist movement that played such a prominent role in the intellectual life of New England in the decades prior to the outbreak of the American Civil War. There is some historical debate about who came up with the name "transcendentalist." It is possible that a member of the movement did, but it is perhaps more likely that it was coined by those who found the group slightly ridiculous and used the impressive fifty-cent word in the spirit of gentle mockery. Edgar Allan Poe, who was never a member of the movement, went well beyond gentle mockery when he dubbed the transcendentalists as "the believers in all things odd."

There was more than a grain of truth in Poe's jibe. The American progressive movement, which began with the Sage of Concord and his curious set of friends, would go on to embrace a variety of different causes between the 1840s and today. But a constant theme of progressivism has been the tendency to champion causes that at the time seemed odd to the average man and woman, and sometimes not just odd but whacko, and even dangerous.

The transcendentalists themselves, and their progressive heirs, were of course quite aware that their ideas struck ordinary people as odd. They would have expected nothing else from the masses of the unenlightened, all of whom were stuck in the rut of habit and custom, resistant to innovation, angered by the very thought that they should change their ways. Mired in the hoary traditions of the past, they were blind to what the transcendentalists could see so clearly before them: a glorious future that awaited a perfected mankind. All that was needed to reach this goal was for the world to follow the advice of the transcendentalists.

But what exactly did they believe?

Perhaps it is best to start with what they could no longer believe. Emerson was raised in the Unitarian tradition, his father being a prominent minister in that quintessentially New England faith. After graduating from Harvard Divinity School, Emerson was ordained as a minister in 1829. He then became the minister of Boston's historic Second Church, where a bit over a century earlier Cotton Mather had preached the traditional Calvinist doctrines. Emerson was soon to discover that even liberal Unitarianism could not be squared with his own conscience, and in 1832 he resigned from his ministry, explaining to his disappointed congregation that he could no longer accept the Unitarian practice of Holy Communion.

Emerson later explained this decision in an essay entitled "The Lord's Supper." Here, Emerson quickly reviews all the various arguments, doctrines, and positions put forth on the subject, from the earliest days of Christianity to his own time, noting how they contradicted one another.

In the Roman Catholic Church, there was the doctrine of transubstantiation, asserting that the bread and wine held in the hands of the priest were miraculously changed into the body and blood of Christ. At the other extreme were those who considered Holy Communion as simply a symbolic reminder of the original Last Supper. Emerson then sums up by writing, "These views of the original account of the Lord's Supper led me to esteem it an occasion full of solemn and prophetic interest, but never intended by Jesus to be the foundation of a perpetual institution."

Emerson is saying that Holy Communion, in one form or another, was been observed by virtually all varieties of the Christian faith, but the mere fact that it is a universally venerated tradition does not really matter. So what does? For Emerson, the critical point lay in his conclusion that Jesus did not *intend* to make it a perpetual institution.

This is not a theological argument but a historical one. Indeed, to probe the psychology of Jesus in order to discover what He intended is the province of historical biography, much like asking whether Julius Caesar really intended to make himself king of Rome. Looking at the available evidence, namely the accounts in the four Gospels, Emerson concludes that while the "occasion" was "full of solemn and prophetic interest," the traditional reading of it was totally wrong, and that all the Christians who thought they were celebrating a rite established by Jesus were in error—though Emerson was not the kind of man to condemn them for adhering to their musty old ideas.

Emerson's break with his Unitarian congregation is a perfect illustration of the enormous impact that German higher criticism of the Bible was having on those who, like Emerson himself, had become familiar with it. Indeed, his essay "The Lord's Supper" provides an excellent sample of both the intentions and methods of this school.

To begin with, all these German scholars were Protestants, which was no accident. The Roman Catholic Church had never hesitated to acknowledge that its doctrines were derived both from scripture and from tradition. What if the doctrine of Purgatory was not spelled out anywhere in the Bible? It was backed by traditional authority, as was the celebration of the Lord's Supper. But it was precisely the Roman Catholic Church's accumulated mass of doctrines backed only by tradition that the Protestant Biblical scholar wanted to eliminate.

Suppose we find a painting from a thousand years ago. It was once the most beautiful painting in the world, we have been told, but over the course of the years many different and inferior hands had attempted to "improve" it by adding bits of color here and there, and even covering the original faces with ones of their own design. Finally, the original painting has been so obscured that it is impossible now even to guess what it looked like when it was first completed. If we want to see the original picture, we will need to hire those who are experts at restoring old paintings to their pristine glory. These men must have special tools and highly developed techniques to do their job well: professionals, not amateurs.

The German Protestant scholars were such professionals. They had received the severe and rigorous education that came to characterize the German universities of the nineteenth century. They had mastered all the languages of the ancient world, not just Latin and Greek, but Aramaic and Syrian. Their objective was simply to restore the original painting that been effaced over time, largely by the Roman Catholic Church with its disfiguring set of traditions. In this respect, they were merely carrying to its logical conclusion what Martin Luther had started back in the days of the Reformation, when he made his great clarion call to return to the texts of the Bible, and only those texts. The Protestant Biblical critics truly believed they were doing the Lord's work with their scholarship.

What became known as the search for the historic Jesus was underway. From the early nineteenth century until today, this search would be called off and then revived again. It fell out of fashion in the middle of the twentieth century but has recently come back into vogue. It was the first wave of critical biblical scholarship, however, that was to have an impact on both European and American thinkers that future waves would never match. As those first Protestant scholars diligently worked to scrape away all the adventitious encrustations that had defaced the original painting, they revealed more and more of a canvas that was not at all what they had expected. Martin Luther himself had held to the orthodox views on the Incarnation and the Trinity. He had held the Lord's Supper to be a sacred tradition, and though he rejected the Catholic doctrine of transubstantiation, he held to the view that Christ was "really present" at the Eucharist, and, of course, he never for a moment questioned that Jesus of Nazareth had performed miracles.

The most decisive break with tradition came with the publication of *The Life of Jesus Critically Examined* by David Friedrich Strauss in 1835. A Protestant theologian who had been trained at the University of Tübingen, Strauss's book challenged everything Protestants had hitherto accepted as articles of faith. Jesus was not divine. He was an ordinary human being, like us. He did not perform miracles; they too were simply part of the disfiguring distortions that had been added to the original canvas.

Emerson had left his congregation three years before Strauss's *Life of Jesus* was published, and fourteen years before George Eliot would publish her translation of Strauss into English. Yet the spirit of the times, which Strauss symbolized, had already led many to look askance at the miracles of Jesus, including Emerson and other members of the New England intellectual elite. But if you take away a belief in these miracles, what is left of the Unitarian faith? Unitarians had argued that these miracles were the proofs that Jesus, while not the Son of God, nevertheless had been sent on a Divine Mission.

In trying to get a grasp on the American transcendentalist movement, it is futile to seek out a common philosophy, even less an ideology. In no sense was it a school of thought, such as Marxism or logical empiricism, where, despite personal variations, there always remained a hard core of central beliefs. Those who became its most prominent members—like Bronson Alcott, Henry David Thoreau, Orestes Brownson, Margaret Fuller, and Theodore Parker—would all eventually go in their own very different directions. Brownson, one of the most brilliant of them all, would convert to the Roman Catholic faith in 1844, after having been raised as a Presbyterian in accordance with strict Calvinist doctrines, then flirting with Unitarianism.

All the New England transcendentalists had something in common: having lost faith in the religion in which they were brought up, they were all seekers after something that would offer them a new faith to take the place of the old. They all wanted something big to believe in. None of them thought even for a moment of simply turning atheist, and Thomas Huxley had not yet coined the term *agnostic*. Far from turning against religion in general, they were trying to find, or create, a new religion that would satisfy their deepest spiritual longings.

Emerson acknowledged his debt to other religious traditions. Like his friend Thoreau, he read and appreciated the Bhagavad Gita and had studied the sacred texts of other nations. He respected their prophets, holy men, and teachers. Yet, as he admits in one of his lectures, Jesus of Nazareth remained for him, as for the other transcendentalists, the supreme educator of mankind. But ultimately, for Emerson, every human being was capable of finding the truth for himself, as he explained in one of his most famous lectures, "Self-Reliance."

On a trip to Europe that Emerson made as a young man, he encountered many of the intellectual luminaries of his time, but by far the greatest influence on his thinking came from the Scottish sage Thomas Carlyle. It was owing to Carlyle that Emerson discovered the German philosopher who would have the greatest influence on the transcendentalist movement: Immanuel Kant. Emerson invokes Kant in his essay "The Transcendentalist," in which he traces the name of the movement back to Kant's most famous work, *Critique of Pure Reason*, in which the term *transcendental* is employed in a highly technical sense, in the thorniest section of that very daunting book, a chapter entitled "The Transcendental Deduction of the Categories." It is not clear that Emerson understood exactly what Kant meant by *transcendental*, but Emerson adopted the term for his own purposes, to mean the truth that anyone could discover for himself through Reason—which is certainly not what Kant meant by this term.

The capital *R* is of great significance; it was a proclamation that Reason had been redeemed. The Orthodox Calvinism that had flourished in the New England of an earlier period placed no faith in human reasoning: due to original sin, God's greatest gift to mankind had been thoroughly corrupted. But this distrust of rational thinking had come to an end. It is true that individuals could still pervert that divine gift, but those who were sincere in their quest for truth could rely on their own unaided intuition to arrive at their goal. None of the transcendentalists displayed even an ounce of Hume's skepticism when it came to their vaunted claims for Reason, which they believed was all sufficient not only to control the passions but to guide mankind to a better and brighter future.

In the series of lectures compiled in *On Heroes, Hero Worship, & the Heroic in History*, Thomas Carlyle championed sincerity as the highest virtue—a virtue, moreover, that could cover a multitude of sins. This was apparent in Carlyle's treatment of the Prophet Mohammed. It was commonly assumed by many educated Englishmen of Carlyle's day that the so-called prophet of Islam had been a fraud, and not even a pious one. They believed that Mohammed had convinced his credulous followers that he was receiving divine messages from Allah by placing a pea in his ear and then having a trained bird try to pick it out, making it look as if the bird—or the angel Gabriel disguised as a bird—had been whispering the Koran to him from on high. All of this, and much more, Carlyle rejected. Mohammed was no con man, but he was absolutely convinced that he was chosen to be the messenger of God, who—like the rest of Carlyle's heroes—was redeemed by the sincerity of his convictions.

This emphasis on sincerity can also be traced back to the philosophy of Kant, who wrote in his *Critique of Practical Reason* that the only thing good without qualification was a good will. In evaluating the behavior of another human being, we should not look at the consequences of their actions but at the intention behind them. If the person meant to do good, that was all that really mattered. Even if their act had unforeseen consequences, the mere fact that those consequences were not intended absolved the actor from bearing guilt for what went wrong.

When Emerson resigned his position as minister over the question of Communion, he was demonstrating his sincerity. He had looked into the matter and he had concluded that he could not in good faith continue to preside over the Lord's Supper services. But this was a feature common to all the transcendentalists: the overriding conviction that a person had to be true to himself, to not be swayed or guided by the prejudices and opinions of others—the fundamental concept that Emerson called "self-reliance." By this phrase, Emerson was not referring to the ability to take care of yourself in the workaday world, as in washing your own clothes or cooking your own food—Emerson had servants for that—but making sure that your own soul had discovered the truth for itself, refusing to accept passively either the doctrines and dogmas of old or what passes for conventional wisdom for the masses. Self-reliance was at bottom self-trust.

Fortunately, it was easy to recognize those men and women who were indeed seeking their own truth. They were those who refused to accept other people's ideas of the truth: "If a man does not keep pace with his companions, perhaps it is because he hears a different drummer," as Emerson's friend, Henry David Thoreau expressed in a memorable aphorism. Another way to put it is that you can recognize someone's sincerity by his eccentric behavior. It was also the way that most people recognized the members of the transcendentalist movement: they were startled and sometimes even shocked by their eccentricity, both in the ideas they held and in their manner of life.

"The mass of men lead lives of quiet desperation," Thoreau observes near the beginning of his most famous book, *Walden*. This was obviously not the case with Thoreau and his transcendentalist friends, who led lives of devoted truth-seeking, listening to that different drummer of theirs. But such a contemptuous attitude toward ordinary men and women had two serious implications, both of which were to infect the American progressive movement with the twin vices of self-conceit and self-deception. Both were pathological variations of the theme of self-trust, that is to say, an excessive trust in the purity of one's own good intentions, hubris disguised as sincerity.

The concept of self-trust represented the most extreme reaction possible to Calvinism, which insisted nothing was more untrustworthy than our egos. Yet, ironically, by dividing the human race into those who were sincere seekers of the truth and those who mindlessly followed the customs and traditions in which they were raised, the transcendentalists were reviving, in a new key, the old Calvinist division between the regenerate and the unregenerate, the elect and the reprobate. Among the transcendentalists, the experience of being "born again" came about when seekers found their own truth and began marching to their own different drummers—a fact that permitted fellow seekers to recognize each other. Like their Puritan ancestors, the transcendentalists constituted an elite—a secular version of the elect who regarded outsiders much as their forefathers had regarded them: as lost souls. As for themselves, this new elite held to the principle "by their fruits, ye shall know them," though this was not merely a metaphor in the case of the New England transcendentalists but was applied literally.

Fad diets are a commonplace of modern life, and the boomers among us can easily recollect dozens of such fads, many of which they have no doubt tried themselves. But for Bronson Alcott, the father of Louisa May Alcott, the right diet was not only healthy but spiritually uplifting—no animal meat nor any animal product. The term *vegan* had yet to be coined, but its principles were already being applied. Yet even today's strictest vegans would be frowned upon by Bronson Alcott and his followers, since modern vegans contaminate both body and soul with those obviously inferior vegetables, like potatoes and carrots, that grow underground—a blatant sign of their unworthiness, in contrast to the vegetables that aspire to the source of light on top of the soil, like cauliflower and brussels sprouts. Obviously the most transcendental diet possible would come from noble trees whose tips came closest to the heavens: fruit trees.

In May 1843, Charles Lane, an English fellow seeker, came to New England to form an ideal community with Bronson Alcott. Lane purchased ninety acres of land in Harvard, Massachusetts, twenty-five miles from Boston. It is true that money changed hands in this transaction—$1,800 of

Lane's money, since his partner Alcott had none—but the idea of vulgarly owning property, like ordinary men, was abhorrent to Alcott's spiritual sensibility. When Alcott informed his friends of his new venture through the medium of their own transcendental magazine, *The Dial*, he underscored this fact by writing, "We have made an arrangement with the proprietor of an estate of about a hundred acres, which *liberates* this tract from human ownership" (emphasis added). It is hard to get more woke than that.

The liberated farm was christened, as one might guess, Fruitlands, though the name embodied a great deal more of wishful thinking than hard reality. The acreage contained ten decrepit apple trees, a house in even worse condition, and a barn. Only about a tenth of the land was fit for growing anything other than ignoble weeds. Further complications arose from Alcott's insistence that no animal should be oppressed by being forced to do the work on the farm—that was what his wife and four young daughters were for. Nor was it deemed permissible to use the excrement of animals to fertilize the gardens—that would constitute theft of the animals' property. Not to mention the degrading nature of the manure itself, hardly fitting for the production of heaven-aspiring veggies and fruits.

This great experiment, undertaken to offer mankind a model of harmonious, simple, and serene communal life, managed to attract six members other than Lane and Alcott and his family. These were a suitably eccentric lot, including Samuel Bower, who believed that clothes were spiritually corrupting and who went around in the nude. Samuel Larned, another seeker, wore clothes but believed that a pure spirit like himself should be able to speak any words that filled his heart, no matter how filthy or obscene. Abraham Everett, who had once been in an insane asylum, was another inmate of Fruitlands and no doubt enjoyed the change of scenery.

The farm did not make it through its first harsh New England winter. There were many reasons for the failure, but prominent among them was the penchant of both Alcott and Lane to travel to Boston and New York to give lectures on the glories of the utopia they had established, leaving Alcott's wife and daughters on the broken-down farm to eke out a subsistence diet on the miserable acreage that Bronson Alcott had expected to be a light unto the worldly gentiles. Later in her life, his daughter Louisa May Alcott penned a short and amusing account of her family's misadventures there, entitled "Transcendental Wild Oats," though she would continue to worship her improvident father, whose very distant drummer kept him marching in every direction except toward any form of gainful employment.

Yet Bronson Alcott should not be dismissed as merely another crackpot, though he was certainly that as well. The great Emerson was not alone in admiring the brilliance of Bronson Alcott's conversational gifts. He could hold some of the finest minds of his time spellbound by the flow of his ideas. When he was urged to submit his writings to *The Dial*, however, they turned out to be vaporous outpourings that struck even his most sympathetic admirers as a trifle insipid. But his one true gift was as an educator.

Before he embarked on the ill-fated Fruitlands fiasco, he had gained a reputation as a pioneer in progressive methods of educating children. In September 1834, he opened a school in Boston, with classes held at the Masonic Temple, from which it derived its name: the Temple School. Dissatisfied with the traditional methods of teaching, which involved mostly learning by rote and drill, Alcott was influenced by European educational reformers such as Pestalozzi. Alcott engaged his pupils in conversations—his strong suit—in order to draw out their own thoughts and ideas, though many of these invariably ended up sounding quite a bit like Alcott's own thoughts and ideas. Yet he deserves credit as the father of the American tradition of the "school trip," as he would take his students to the country and let them explore nature under his guidance.

Scandal, however, erupted when his assistant, one of the famous Peabody sisters, published an account of his teaching methods, which indicated that Alcott probed his pupils on such questions as whether the miracles recounted in the Gospel had really taken place. He was quickly denounced by more conservative Bostonians, and the school soon had no pupils to teach. Yet Peabody's book made it to England, where it was hailed by truth-seekers there, including Charles Lane, who—inspired by Alcott's educational ideas—crossed the Atlantic to join Alcott in establishing their misguided utopia.

Emerson visited Fruitlands only once and was sensible enough to doubt its long tenure, especially come winter. His own experiments in living were far more modest, though no more successful. Feeling uneasy about the status of his servants, Emerson once decided that they should start taking their meals with him and his wife each evening—an experiment that was soon terminated at his servants' request and never repeated. Transcendental table talk was apparently not to their taste.

In her most famous novel, *Little Women*, Louisa May Alcott explains the poverty of her family's life by saying that their father had lost his wealth because he had tried to help a friend in need, pledging security for a debt that in the end he had to pay himself, thereby bankrupting him and impoverishing his entire family. In truth, Bronson Alcott felt that his calling was too lofty to be degraded by any sordid commercial labor, an attitude that was also shared by fellow seeker Henry David Thoreau, whose writings are marked by the insufferable self-conceit of the man who preens himself on his superior independence of mind, while sneering at those who are satisfied with an ordinary life of family and work.

Such self-conceit leads to the second vice of self-deception. The New England Calvinists of old were challenged by the problem of hypocrisy: an individual may behave to all outward appearances as one of the divinely elected saints, but it is always possible that this might be merely a pose designed to fool others. The neo-Puritan elite of the transcendentalists faced a similar problem. Just as the hypocrite can imitate the life of the sanctified in his behavior, so a rogue may pretend to be a seeker by merely acting eccentric. Even more worrisome were those who believed that the mere display of eccentricity was enough to secure their place among the transcendentalist elect, and even worse were those for whom eccentricity becomes an end in itself, not the byproduct of a search for a higher truth— at which point such individuals will inevitably be seduced into thinking they are wiser than ordinary men and women, simply because they are odder. Bronson Alcott perhaps best summed up the movement by referring to it as "the Newness." There is self-evident danger in making an idol of the merely new and the merely odd, since there is an enormous range of eccentric behavior that is merely stupid, a factor that we will examine in further detail when we come to an analysis of American progressivism in our own day.

The transcendentalists were not skeptics. If anything, they tended to believe too much rather than too little, including a belief in spirits and a taste for the mystical speculations of Emanuel Swedenborg. They wallowed in vague but lofty abstractions. Though many of them could no longer accept orthodox Christianity, they were all deeply convinced that their ideals were bound to triumph, because they were also God's ideals. They also believed that God was slowly but surely bringing these ideals to fruition in the historical arena. Jehovah had led the children of Israel out of the House of Bondage in the Egypt of old, and who could doubt that He would lead the children of Africa out of the House of Bondage that had been established in the slave states of the Old South? God was clearly and manifestly on their side. And, as we have seen, they also believed He was on the side of their hero, John Brown.

Yet in their celebration of John Brown, Emerson and Thoreau remained true to the transcendental principle that what mattered about a man was the sincerity of his convictions, not the consequences of his actions. No one had ever questioned John Brown's sincerity—what fanatic is without it? He was deeply devoted to a genuinely noble cause—that of freeing the long-suffering slaves—and admirable in death, and that was enough for the transcendentalists. Why be concerned about the horrendous consequences that his actions might have unleashed? The idea, ultimately derived from Kant's maxim that the only thing that was good without qualification was a good will, had been channeled to Emerson and his circle via Thomas Carlyle's elevation of sincerity to the highest virtue obtainable. In Emerson's most famous essay, "Self-Reliance," Carlylean sincerity became self-trust.

The twentieth century would see the assumption of enormous power by men overflowing with self-trust, fanatically sincere in their conviction that, like the transcendentalists, they were ushering in a new age, a future radically different from the past, which they alone had been chosen by history to bring into being. Their devout followers regarded them as Carlylean Heroes and Great Men, though the later verdict of history has been less favorable to their reputation. Indeed, today the names of Vladimir Lenin and Adolf Hitler, Benito Mussolini and Josef Stalin, evoke not the sincerity of their intentions but the appalling consequences of their actions.

We will now look at another innovation that the transcendentalists introduced into American society, an import from Europe like so many of the other ideas embraced by the New England cult of advanced thinkers: socialism.

CHAPTER SEVEN

SOCIALISM COMES TO AMERICA

Brook Farm was by far the most famous experiment in communal living in nineteenth-century New England. The land on which it was founded was purchased in 1841, and it managed to hang on to life until 1846. Its founder, George Ripley, was inspired by the ideals current among his fellow transcendentalists, who hoped that Brook Farm would provide all the necessities of life with minimal labor, allowing its residents to devote their abundance of leisure time to more uplifting activities. Unfortunately, this proved to be a pipe dream, though marginally more successful than the utter debacle that was Fruitlands.

Nathaniel Hawthorne, who had joined the commune and would later write his novel *The Blithedale Romance* based on his experience there, complained about the hard work that all were expected to perform on the farm, writing that "labor is the curse of the world, and nobody can meddle with it without becoming proportionately brutified." The always more level-headed Emerson was asked to join Brook Farm but declined. He anticipated what would invariably be the downfall of any communal experiment, no matter how well-intentioned. There would always be free-loaders who "looked out the window all day," while others were busy laboring in the fields, and yet the free-loader invariably expected to have equal shares in the fruits of other people's toil. Henry David Thoreau, the quintessential loner, also felt that Brook Farm was no place for him.

In 1844, Brook Farm decided to adopt the principles of the French socialist Charles Fourier, whose ideas were then at the peak of their influence. At that time, when people thought of socialism, they usually meant Fourierism—Karl Marx and Friedrich Engels would not publish *The Communist Manifesto* until 1848. What made the Brook Farm experiment so significant is that it was here, for the first time, that European socialism was introduced to America, though there had been previous experiments in communal living.

The first Shaker villages had been established in New England in the late seventeenth century, and they would outlive by many generations both Brook Farm and Fruitlands. The sect was founded by English prophetess Ann Lee, who believed that the traditional family was the source of conflict and discord, and hence required all her followers to take vows of celibacy. Though unable to produce children of their own, the Shakers survived by acquiring new converts to their simple way of life. Today, the Sabbathday Lake Shaker Village in Maine is the home of the two or three remaining members of this sect—by far the oldest experiment in communal living on record, outside of Catholic and Orthodox monasteries.

Celibacy was not one of Charles Fourier's requirements for those who joined his community. On the contrary, it was whispered that life in his utopian communes was pretty much a sexual free-for-all, with neither incest nor homosexuality being off the table. While Fourier was the most influential socialist before Marx, he was by no means alone in his ambition to alter man's future one commune at a time. Indeed, ever since the word *socialisme* had been coined by Pierre Leroux, a French philosopher of the nineteenth century, the term has taken on a bewildering variety of meanings. Christian socialism, Romantic socialism, anarchic socialism, and scientific socialism are but some of the more prominent varieties. Yet there are a number of basic features that they share.

In earlier centuries, a number of individual thinkers had devised imaginary societies that would be free from the flaws that marred the real world.

The differences between rich and poor would disappear. Through the abolition of private property, all members of the ideal society would share everything in common. Obviously, there could be no civil strife or war in a community in which all sources of conflict had been eliminated, so harmony would prevail among all individuals, and no war would disturb their serenity. Nor would the ideal community need to worry about foreign aggressors, not because world peace had finally been established, but due to a feature that was essential to all the utopian schemes: the absence of neighbors.

The most famous was Plato's Republic, in which there was considerable elaboration of the details that would govern this ideal city-state. It was to be set on a remote island where it would not need to deal with either overt enemies or with cultural influences that could seduce the citizens of the republic with the blandishments of alien ways. To use Karl Popper's phrase, Plato's Republic was to be an emphatically "closed society." This same principle would apply to the ideal societies of later ages—Francis Bacon's New Atlantis, Tommaso Campanella's City of the Sun, and Thomas More's Utopia (from whose name this genre of literature was derived) were all located on remote islands.

The one curious exception to this rule was the novel *The Year 2440* by Louis-Sébastien Mercier, published in 1771, which differs from all previous utopias in several significant ways. Instead of being set in a remote and unknown island, the story takes place in Paris, but a Paris that is nearly seven centuries distant from the date of the novel's publication. The visitor does not arrive there by boat but merely by falling asleep, only to wake up to a Paris that has been utterly transformed. Gone are the vices, filth, wickedness, and inequities that characterized the Paris of 1771. There are no longer beggars, monks, prostitutes, priests, soldiers, and criminals in a France that is now ruled by a wise and benevolent philosopher-king à la Plato.

Yet there is a jarring note to Mercier's vision. It is as if seven hundred years of progress had achieved nothing more than a return to ancient Sparta, only a more severe one. Indeed, in surveying the utopian literature of the past, going all the way back to Plato's Republic, it is hard to miss a theme common to them all, namely an idealization of the Spartan way of life, with its emphasis on simplicity and regimentation. The influence of Jean-Jacques Rousseau on Mercier's vision is most evident in its condemnation of those perverted tastes that smack of the overly civilized. In the Paris of 2440, for example, coffee, tea, and tobacco had long been banned as useless and immoral. Also eliminated are dancing masters. The vast majority of books written over the previous centuries had been happily consigned to the flames by the enlightened librarians of the new age, though a small library of choice books remained.

Significantly, the France of the future will have no religion and will be thoroughly secular. Science has now replaced outdated faith, and children are now instructed in the use of scientific instruments, such as microscope and telescopes, instead of memorizing the catechism in preparation for their first Communion. This last note clearly marks Mercier as an adherent of the more radical and anti-Christian wing of the French Enlightenment. In his anticipation of a better world in the distant future, Mercier struck a chord of historical optimism that no other figure of the Enlightenment had sounded until Condorcet's treatise on the perfectibility of man, published twenty-three years later.

Mercier's novel has often been seen as one of the pioneering works of the genre that became known as science fiction. Prior to the publication of *The Year 2440*, there had been scattered and tentative allusions to the future in various works, but no one had ever before set an entire novel in the future—a fact that speaks volumes about the great transformation in mankind's attitude toward the future that was taking place at this time. The American Revolution, with its establishment of a New Order of the Ages, came five years after the publication of Mercier's book, and the French Revolution followed within two decades. Along with it came the attempt to start the historical process afresh from the Year One and efforts to abolish religion to create a society based on Reason alone.

Yet how seriously did Mercier take his own vision? In French, the full title of his novel is *L'An 2440, rêve s'il en fut jamais*, which is normally translated as *The Year 2440, a dream if there ever was one.* The subtitle refers to the story's setting as a dream, but it also suggests that Mercier was self-consciously indulging in a fantasy of an ideal society, differing from earlier utopian visions only by being set not on a remote island but in the far-distant future. In short, it did not offer itself as a practical guide to how the men of his own time might go about constructing a perfect society in the here and now.

In sharp contrast, for the socialists of the nineteenth century, utopia was not merely a fantasy ideal but a precisely engineered blueprint that would be realized in their generation down to the last detail. Nor were these utopias to be cut off from the rest of the world. They were not like the land of Shangri-La, invented by English novelist James Hilton as the setting of his 1933 adventure novel, *Lost Horizon*, where a small group of human beings created a perfect society in the midst of the Himalayas—a paradise on earth, as the novel makes clear, that is only the stuff that dreams are made of. Though some of the socialists had visions of the future that were far more fanciful than anything available to the denizens of Shangri-La, they were certainly not seen as fantasies by their proponents or followers.

The nineteenth-century socialists were not interested in establishing geographically isolated and solitary enclaves on faraway islands or in secluded valleys. For them, socialism was nothing less than the Wave of the Future, which in time would come to engulf the entire globe, drawing in all mankind, from every race, creed, and color, by virtue of its obvious blessings. Furthermore, once socialism had been achieved, there would be no need to look for a further stage of development, because the inherently progressive movement of history had achieved its consummation. The future after socialism would simply be more and better socialism, possibly including the transition to the end goal toward which all previous ages were groping: namely the ideal communist society, in which everyone's needs and desires were fully and richly met with only the most minimal effort on everyone's part. "From each according to his abilities, to each according to his needs," as the famous adage goes.

Essential to any Fourierist commune was a *phalanstery*, a neologism coined by Fourier to describe the large barrack/dormitory in which the member of his socialist commune would work, play, and sleep. The French word *phalanstère* was a combination of *phalange*, the French word for the Greek term *phalanx*, and *monastère*, the French word for *monastery*. The term *phalanx* referred to the tight, highly organized body of armed men that was believed to have originated in ancient Sparta; the idealized glamor of Sparta endured even among the nineteenth century socialists. Fourier's idea of the phalanstery echoed the barrack/dormitory in which all Spartan males were required to live until the age of thirty. Even the gentle transcendentalists of New England admired Spartan virtues, and this no doubt played a role in their adopting Fourier's system after the early mistrials and errors of Brook Farm's initial years.

Marx and Engels would later insist that the coming of socialism would require a violent revolution. The capitalist class would not relinquish its power unless it was forced to do so by its class enemies, the proletariat. This naturally raised the question of what to do with the capitalists after the revolution, since they would continue to pose an internal threat; none of the prospects for them was pleasant.

Fourierism required neither revolution nor coercion. When the world began to notice how wonderfully prosperous, happy, and harmonious Fourier's socialist communities were, both capitalists and laborers would want start their own. An English follower of Charles Fourier argued that the rapid spread of these phalansteries would be akin to the rapid expanse of the recently invented railroad. Once people saw the advantages of traveling by rail, as opposed to horse-drawn carriages, they would immediately begin to clamor for the construction of more and more railways to more and more different destinations. So, the phalanstery system would triumph quite naturally and without any effort at deliberate propagation. Here disciples of Fourier would work for each other's mutual benefit and satisfaction, while the rest of the world would marvel at their blissful existence and would forthwith commence to set up their own phalansteries, spreading socialistic harmony across the globe, one phalanstery at a time.

As soon as the residents of Brook Farm decided to adopt the Fourier model, they borrowed money to build a phalanstery of their own. Unfortunately, the phalanstery burned down while it was still under construction and left a sizeable debt to be paid off. Like the orphanage in Ibsen's *Ghosts*, it had not been insured, though it is not clear whether this omission was due to a trust in Divine Providence or simple transcendental negligence. At all events, the Brook Farm experiment that had begun so hopefully now lay in both literal and metaphorical ashes.

Considering the failure of Brook Farm and many other Fourier-inspired communities, it seems incredible that so many intelligent men and women took the ideas of Charles Fourier seriously. Among his more startling prophecies was that this marvelous transformation of human life would result in changes to the physical composition of the earth, until one day the salt oceans of the world would be turned into lemonade. (No joke.)

As those of us who do not live in a phalanstery may have noticed, or even those who have gotten a mouthful of saltwater while swimming in the sea, Fourier's visions of the future did not come to pass. Yet there can be no question that his ideas caught on like wildfire among those of his contemporaries who longed for a world in which the gross inequalities of the capitalist system could be overcome by a more equitable living arrangement designed to promote social harmony and social justice. Indeed, so attractive was Fourier's ideal that even today there are those who believe the time has come to revive his ideals, even creating a website to promote them.

Today, it is hard to suppress the feeling that a man who believed the oceans would turn into lemonade was either a lunatic or a charlatan. Tempting as it is to draw such a conclusion, to underestimate the sincerity of socialist thinkers, both past and present, is to court disaster—they were absolutely sincere, often to the point of fanaticism. To dismiss them as quacks and daydreamers is misguided, for it ignores the enormous impact the socialist ideal has had on the real world, and which it not only continues to have but which might become more potent in the coming years.

It is also of equal importance to recall that the nineteenth-century capitalist system attacked by Karl Marx and the other socialists of his time was not the same capitalist system that has come into existence since the end of the Second World War. Even the leading British Marxist of our day, David Harvey, has referred to this latter system as "the Great Moderation"—a period in which capitalism achieved both economic growth and a reasonably fair distribution of rewards, subject only to mild ups and downs, without the severe crises which had previously been endemic to it. It is too easy for us to engage in the forgetfulness in which we assume that the past was little different from the present. To forget the brutal conditions of the nineteenth-century working class is to miss the reason so many men and women of compassion, intelligence, and good sense turned so hopefully to the promises made by the socialists of that era. Many of these utopian socialists were quite well off and were not motivated by envy. They certainly were not looking for welfare checks from the government, but were intent on providing for their own needs through their own productive labor in their little communes. Nor were these utopian socialists primarily motivated by altruism, as the followers of Ayn Rand are fond of arguing. The utopians were seeking a world in which they would be happier themselves, and if this world of their little utopian community made other people happy as well, this was just an additional benefit.

It is also easy to forget that socialism, though it had its origins in Europe, became a popular cause among the educated elite in the United States, especially toward the end of the nineteenth century. One of the most popular books of that era, selling over a million copies, was the novel *Looking Backward: 2000–1887* by Edward Bellamy. Appearing in 1888, it was an instant smash success. Of all the books published in nineteenth-century America, only *Uncle Tom's Cabin* sold more copies in its first year. Bellamy's novel was also wildly successful in England, and within three years of its initial appearance, translators in China were busy preparing their own edition for the Celestial Kingdom. Yet Bellamy's book was far more than a mere bestseller. It was a book with a message, and its message was enthusiastically embraced by its millions of readers. It showed vividly what a gleaming paradise awaited Americans in the future.

Like Harriet Beecher Stowe's famous book, *Looking Backward* was not intended to be read and then discarded, like the average novel of the time. Both novels were intended to cause a stir, and in this respect both succeeded beyond their authors' most sanguine dreams. While historians may dispute the legend about President Lincoln's meeting with Mrs. Stowe, most would agree with the spirit of his famous quip: "So you are the little woman who wrote the book that started this great war." Although Bellamy's book did not start even a small war, it did initiate a political movement both in America and abroad. Within a few years of its appearance, there were 162 Bellamy Clubs, as they were called, in the USA—all devoted to the propagation of the vision of the future that the book presented.

The nineteenth century had witnessed a steady flow of socialist tracts and pamphlets, written in virtually every European language, some published openly and others clandestinely. In addition, there were huge tomes, written in elegant and clever French or ponderous German, articulating different visions of man's socialist future. The great prophet of scientific socialism, Karl Marx, had finished the final volume of his gigantic treatise *Das Kapital* only a few years before Bellamy's book. A challenge to read in any language, with its three volumes running to over three thousand pages, Marx's *opus magnum* was looked upon by his followers as the sacred scripture of socialism, yet its value as pure entertainment has never been regarded as highly, even by its most ardent admirers. The same could not be said of Bellamy's book. It was a genuine novel, a kind of romance, with a plot and reasonably convincing characters, which not only engaged the readers of the late nineteenth century but continues to do so today (check out the many glowing reviews of the book on Amazon, posted within the last few years).

Today, *Looking Backward* is classified as utopian literature, and it certainly belongs there, but it resembles Sebastian Mercier's *The Year 2440* in two respects. It is not set on a desert island nor in a hidden valley, but in prosaic Boston. The protagonist of the tale, an affluent but dyspeptic proper Bostonian, Julian West, goes to sleep one night in the year 1887 and awakens in the year 2000—only 113 years later, compared to the elapse of nearly four centuries in Mercier's novel. Bellamy even has a chapter in which Julian West "awakes" to find that it has all been a dream, and that he has been returned to the bleak and dismal Boston of his own day. Fortunately, this "awakening" turns out to have been nothing more than a nightmare, and he rejoices to find himself once more in the marvelous world of the future.

Stunned to wake up in a world in which everyone is blissfully happy, West is naturally curious to discover how this miraculous transformation has been achieved. Fortunately, he is provided with a guide, the venerable Dr. Leete, who explains how it all came about. To begin with, the advent of socialism had not been brought about by a violent revolution, as orthodox Marxism required. Class conflict, the motor of Marx's theory of history, also played no role in its creation. Furthermore, the impetus behind the new socialist order was not the desire to help out the poor or the oppressed, and it had nothing in common with the welfare state and its aims.

Julian West had been a very wealthy man back in 1887, but he discovers in the new socialist order that there is no need of personal wealth in order to enjoy the good things of life, which are now abundantly available to all. According to Dr. Leete, at some point in the past, Americans of all classes had reached a virtually unanimous agreement that the capitalist system needed to be replaced with a new way of life, one in which the economic order had been fully rationalized. A national industrial army had come into being in which everyone was required to work until the age of forty-five. There would still be menial jobs that needed to be performed, but these would be shared by all, rather than reserved for a specific class. Hence, such work involved no stigma and would not require much energy and effort, since everyone would do their fair share of it.

It should be remembered that in 1887 the rich invariably had servants, often quite a few of them, to handle the menial tasks in their own homes:

housekeeping, garbage removal, laundry, greeting visitors, and food purchasing, preparation, and cooking. In Bellamy's America of 2000, however, there was no need to go to the trouble of preparing meals for oneself or family, since there was a multitude of large restaurants managed by the state, offering a variety of dishes, where everyone invariably preferred to dine. The underlying assumption here is that no one could possibly want to go to the trouble to cook for themselves—a notion that strikes most of us as strange today, given the culinary revolution in America during the last half-century that began with Julia Child; once seen as a drudgery, cooking has become an enjoyable pastime for many. But Bellamy's elimination of the need to cook for oneself represented the utopian idealist's vision of a world largely freed from menial tasks. Of course, there were still forms of labor that were both physically demanding and often dangerous, but those employed in these fields would have shorter hours and a higher rate of compensation than those who worked at lighter and less demanding jobs. Fairness was the general principle, thereby assuring a society in which no one had cause to complain about their lot.

Bellamy is not a science fiction writer, and he does not indulge in flights of technological fancy—no rockets to the moon or flying cars. Yet he brilliantly extrapolates from the innovations of his time. The telephone, which had been invented only eleven years before Julian West fell asleep, has been ennobled to serve the purposes of higher culture. Houses in 2000 have special rooms where one can listen to any of four different "stations," each of which carries a different kind of classical music. (However, Bellamy did not foresee the advent of LPs or CDs. Each of his different channels is connected by telephone line to live performers at the other end. Later, in the real America of the 1920s, the early proponents of radio believed that the chief mission of this new invention would be to bring Beethoven and Wagner to the masses.)

In Bellamy's era, there was a budding movement toward consumer cooperatives where the buyer could purchase goods directly from those who produced them, thereby eliminating the need for a middleman, who was looked upon as an unnecessary cog in the machine and who should be dispensed with in the name of economic rationality. In Bellamy's future world, the cooperative principle has been extended to every aspect of commercial life. Shopping too has been rationalized: the consumer merely selects from a menu of items available and pays with something akin to a credit or debit card. The item is then promptly delivered to her door, with Amazon-like efficiency. Poverty has of course been eliminated, and with it most types of crime. Yet a stubborn criminal element still remains; for Bellamy, these individuals represent throwbacks to a more primitive time, and they receive medical treatment for their atavistic tendencies. Later American progressives would include mandatory sterilization as an essential part of their "medical" treatment.

If Bellamy could awaken from his own long sleep and observe the America of today, what would he make of it? There are now a number of different companies that provide streaming music services, allowing you to choose from not just four different channels but to access literally millions of different performances of an astonishing variety of musical genres, many of which might certainly have shocked Bellamy's classical tastes. Amazon has managed to eliminate millions of middlemen, and can deliver almost anything you desire to your front door with only a click of a button. Yet these and many other innovations were not the result of a peaceful socialist revolution but of the profit motive, which demands the maximum rationalization of the production and distribution of goods if a company wishes to stay competitive. It was capitalism that brought these innovations into being, not socialism.

Bellamy's ideal of socialism has its roots not in Marxism but in America's own tradition of utopian thinking, hearkening back to the idyllic visions of George Ripley and Bronson Alcott. However, in Bellamy's version, it is the entire nation that has been turned into a commune. Strange as it may sound to the progressives of today, Bellamy makes nationalism, not class-conflict, the impetus and the guiding principle for the creation of the new social order. It is the American nation as a whole that has recognized the need for socialist cooperation, and it is justified as being in the national interest. Just as soldiers march off to war, prepared to give their lives for their country, so Bellamy's industrial army goes to work each day in the same spirit of patriotic devotion. Who does not want to see their own beloved nation both more prosperous and harmonious? No one, according to Bellamy, which explains how the revolution came about through class consensus and not through class struggle.

There is a small detail in Bellamy's future America that demonstrates how firmly his ideals are rooted in the homegrown tradition of American utopianism. In addition to classical music, there are also uplifting sermons instantly available via telephone. The Bostonians in Bellamy's year 2000 remain good Christians, as devoted to the preaching of the gospel as their distant Puritan ancestors were. Marx's atheism has no place in Bellamy's future. In the America of the nineteenth century, spiritualism and social-ism were expected to combine forces in creating the utopia of the future.

Bellamy's English contemporary, the socialist Renaissance man William Morris, presents something of an enigma. He claimed to be a Marxist, and yet his own utopian novel, *News from Nowhere*, published only a few years after Bellamy's, exhibits no trace of Marx's influence. When Morris's hero and narrator, William Guest, wakes up after a good night's sleep, he does not immediately realize that he has been magically transported into the distant future. As he wanders down a meadow to the Thames, the first cue that his world has changed dramatically is a nearby bridge. The day before, it had been an ugly iron bridge. Overnight, how-ever, it has been transformed into a beautiful bridge made of intricately carved wood. This is a telling detail; Karl Marx and those who would later put his theories in practice were invariably champions of industrial tech-nology. The Soviets loved huge factories and immense industrial projects. Ford and his assembly line were seen as the wave of progress. To them, it would certainly make sense to tear down an iron bridge and replace it with one made of steel, but to replace it with a wooden bridge? That was a step backward, not forward.

For William Morris, however, the reason for replacing an iron bridge with one made of wood was simple: the wooden bridge was obviously more beautiful. In his own time, as well as in ours, Morris's fame rested on his skill as a designer of gorgeous fabrics, many of which remain popular today. In addition, he was a poet, an artist, and a printer of fine and aesthetically pleasing books. He was also devoted to conserving the architecture of the past, and he would certainly have loathed the brutalist and utilitarian building projects beloved of not only Soviet architects but many in the capitalist nations as well. Mass production, offering cheap goods for the common people, was to Morris an abomination. Instead, he championed the craftsmanship of the old-fashioned artisans, working as individuals or in small groups, who simply aimed to create objects that satisfied their own aesthetic ideals. By the Marxists' standards, this was heresy. Morris's fastidious taste reflected the rarefied atmosphere of the late nineteenth-century English aesthetes like the pre-Raphaelites. It was elitist and reactionary, designed to delight the cultivated, not to serve the masses. No Henry Ford assembly line for William Morris.

As William Guest explores his new world, the masses are conspicuously absent from the scenes he encounters. The men and women that he comes across are all quite educated, like himself, and speak in the style of the gentry. In the new order, however, the gentlefolk enjoy participating in such festivities as harvesting the crops along with the happy agrarian laborers, whom they treat as their fellows. True to every utopian vision of socialism—indeed, one of their cardinal themes—is that what was once despised as undignified forms of labor have been magically transformed into fun activities that no one considers beneath him (or beneath her, for the sexes now are equal).

There are some amusing tidbits in Morris's dream of his socialist future. One of the ladies whom Guest encounters sports a tan; her skin has been bronzed from exposure to the sun. The modern reader finds nothing strange here—that is why we have swimming pools and tanning beds, after all—but it was designed to shock the sensibilities of Morris's Victorian readership. Ladies of that era were distinguished from lower-class women by alabaster white skin, especially their hands and arms, which is why they always wore gloves. Tanned skin, rather than being desired by the affluent, was a mark of those who had to work in the fields—the now happy agrarian laborers formerly known as peasants.

In conversing with his newfound friends, however, William Guest discovers that even utopias have their drawbacks. He learns that though people write novels about the glorious new era that mankind has achieved, few read them. They are simply too dull and, worst of all, predictable. Nearly everyone else prefers to read novels about the bad old days before the sunshine of socialism began to warm every human heart. The characters in the old novels were still plagued by enough day-to-day troubles to make their lives both interesting and unpredictable. Perhaps here we find William Morris the artist poking a bit of fun at William Morris the socialist. If life in utopia is too boring even to read about, might it not be just as boring to live it? After all, the promise of all utopias to make life trouble-free for all, but perhaps it is just our troubles, and overcoming them, that make our lives worth living. How, after all, can life retain its zest in a world in which everything has become predictable?

Although the utopian novels of William Morris and Edward Bellamy are sometimes thought of as specifically Marxist, a careful reader will see the standard tropes of utopian socialism. It is frequently forgotten that Karl Marx himself offered few glimpses of what the socialist future would be like, and those few contradict the quaint visions offered by Bellamy and Morris. Under socialism, according to Marx, labor remained labor, not a hobby for dilettantes. Work would be paid according to how much a person did of it, and how well. Exactly how this would be achieved in detail was left to the future society to decide for itself. Unlike the utopian socialists with their detail blueprints for the future, Marx was remarkably mum on how socialism would actually work in practice. Whether Marx's attitude toward this problem represented a dodging of the issue, or a sensible modesty before the unknown future, is a matter of conjecture, though it is difficult to believe that Marx would have had much use for Morris's genteel socialism or Bellamy's Boston Brahmin version of a socialist nationalism. For Marx, nationalism was an outmoded stage that his own international world order would happily transcend.

Yet William Morris would not be the last man to call himself a Marxist without appearing to have any idea of what Marxism was all about. Many would follow his example, and today the academic world as well as the woke community are full of these faux Marxists. Like the label *progressive*, the label *Marxist* casts a magic spell over those who think of themselves as being on the right side of history. It flatters their self-image, offering them the romance of revolution without seriously endangering the source of their very comfortable lifestyle, which, needless to say, is provided by the vile and despicable system known as capitalism that they allegedly long to overthrow.

Though both Julian West and William Guest travel through time, they do so without a machine. But shortly after their adventures, another Victorian fictional character invents such a marvelous machine and uses it to explore not the future of a century hence but one unimaginably distant from his own day.

The literary genre of the time traveler has long been in vogue, new books with this theme appearing as a dizzying rate each year. If you do a search on who wrote the first book about time travel, the answer will be H. G. Wells, in his justly celebrated novel *The Time Machine*, published in 1895. However, Spanish fans of science fiction will demur, pointing out that eight years earlier, the Spanish diplomat and writer Enrique Lucio Eugenio Gaspar y Rimbau had introduced a time-traveling device in a comic opera (or *zarzuela*) for which he had written the libretto. Both the opera and the time machine were called by the made-up phrase *El ana-crónópete*, which means something like "the thing that flies backwards," and which ends up taking the time traveler not into the distant future but back to the very origin of the universe—all for comic effect, with songs.

The time machine that Wells envisioned in his book could also go backward. But its brilliant inventor had no interest in returning to the past, which was, for him as for many of us today, simply ancient history. What he wanted to see was the future—as Wells himself titled another of his books, *The Shape of Things to Come*. The future was more alluring and more tantalizing—what did it hold for the human race?

Like Edward Bellamy and William Morris, H. G. Wells was a confirmed socialist. Indeed, it would difficult to find even a handful of eminent literary men of that era who were not, in one way or another, self-described socialists. Similarly, his time traveler, who is never given a name in the story, is eager to see if mankind has in fact achieved the promised platitudes of liberty, equality, and fraternity—the social justice for which men like himself had long striven. When his time machine eventually comes to a halt in the year AD 802,701, the protagonist believes this earthly paradise is exactly what he has found. It is full of beautiful young men and women, who sport and gambol in Elysian-like fields, carefree and clearly not wage slaves under the thumb of some brutal capitalist exploiter. At last, the time traveler happily reflects, mankind has entered the Golden Age of its ancient dreams: the long-anticipated socialist paradise where men and women, freed from menial toil, could devote themselves to higher things.

Had Wells ended his novel on this note, it would have taken its place next to Bellamy's *Looking Backward* and Morris's *News from Nowhere*—another engaging utopian fantasy set in the future. But *The Time Machine* doesn't end that way. Instead, Wells offers up the most terrifying dystopian vision ever penned. In George Orwell's vision of the future, *1984*, Big Brother was always watching you, but he wasn't planning to eat you, like the Morlocks in Wells's tale. They are the reason those beautiful youngsters, known as the Eloi, have so much leisure time. They have no need to work because the Morlocks, who dwell underground, look after them, giving them food and clothing and shelter—a bit like the ideal welfare state. Though liberated from the need to work, the Eloi show absolutely no interest in higher things. Ancient libraries contain volumes that turn to dust when touched. There are no arts, no music, no literature—just endless dalliance and frolic in the sun. Even more shocking, all feelings of humanity have vanished among the Eloi. When a beautiful girl accidentally gets caught in a river's strong current and yells for help, her fellow Eloi pay her not the least attention, and it is the protagonist who must save her. Finally, he comes to realize that the welfare state created for the Eloi by the Morlocks is not an altruistic venture. The Morlocks feed and care for the Eloi for the same reason that humans care for their cattle: to fatten them up and eat them.

It is tempting to think that Wells the science fiction writer has glimpsed something that conflicts with his own theories about the socialist future. What would happen to mankind if the Golden Age were to come again? What would become of men if they did not have to labor or struggle, or confront the unexpected and the unpredictable? In a welfare state that clothed and fed everyone and handled all their problems, that made life free from challenge and utterly predictable, how would anyone be able to emerge from the helpless state of infantilism that the Eloi symbolized?

This line of thinking raises the question: Suppose socialism actually *did* work, and exactly as its ardent proponents hoped it would: free from Gulags or purge trials, free from famine and scarcity, just as glorious as William Morris and Edward Bellamy depicted it? How many generations of such carefree life would it take before it began to produce a race of Eloi? It is no accident that, in depicting his Eloi, Wells drew upon the pastoral tropes popularized by Theocritus and Virgil, who filled their verses with beautiful lads and lovely lasses who, like the Eloi, spent insouciant days of endless summer amid their "snakeless meadows, unlaborious earth, and oarless sea." There can always be too much of a good thing, even of Golden Ages—and one that lasts forever might be more than mankind can bear.

Utopian socialism, so popular in the nineteenth century, is still with us today. The Occupy Wall Street movement that made headlines in the fall of 2011 evoked the shades of past utopian schemes: grandiose in ambition but quickly fizzling out due to poor planning and squabbling egos. It lasted a mere fifty-one days, making Bronson Alcott's Fruitlands, which lasted a whole year, look like a smashing success. The woke movement of today breathes the same atmosphere of high-minded impracticality that is the traditional mark of utopian socialists, though many of its advocates seem to be under the delusion that they are Marxists.

Yet Karl Marx, who was about as woke as Miss Manners, had a radically different conception of socialism, rejecting root and branch the vaporous and fantastic daydreams that filled the minds of utopian socialists, before and after his day. It is time to take a look at Marx. It is also high time that conservatives stop telling themselves that he was a faux Santa Claus who promised people "free stuff." Thomas Sowell, the most distinguished conservative intellect of our time, began his career as a Marxist and would later write one of the finest and most sympathetic accounts of Marxism on record. Indeed, it is an open question whether anyone who has not seriously engaged with Karl Marx can begin to understand what is so wrong about "the right side of history."

CHAPTER EIGHT

KARL MARX AND THE MYTH
OF CULTURAL MARXISM

In their efforts to come to grasp with the woke movement of today, many conservative intellectuals have invoked Karl Marx. The term *cultural Marxism* has come into vogue as a way of explaining what the Woke Revolution is all about, especially in relation to critical race theory. After all, when a prominent leader in the Black Lives Matter movement tells the world that she and her colleagues are "highly trained Marxists," shouldn't we take them at their word?

As it turns out, we shouldn't. Again, we must keep in mind the power of labels. Like the label *progressive*, the label *Marxist* has a certain cachet. There is not only the romance of revolution attached to it but also very serious thinking. For Karl Marx, even when he was wrong, was always serious, and perhaps most illuminating precisely when he was the most wrong. But just as all that glitters is not gold, so too all who call themselves Marxists may never have read, much less understood, the dialectical subtleties of *The Communist Manifesto*, not to mention the daunting Mount Everest of all three volumes of *Das Kapital*. If they had, they would be aware that critical race theory is the most blatantly anti-Marxist ideology that has ever been conjured up in the minds of men. But in order to understand what Marxism isn't, we must first try to understand what Marxism is.

As we have seen, there were many socialist theories before the advent of Marx and Engels, offering many different versions of how to go about constructing the ideal community. Almost all of these were small affairs, with at most a few thousand members, where the decision of whether or not to join the commune was left entirely to the individual. While their proponents certainly hoped that their particular model communities would become the wave of the future, none of them claimed that it was certain this would come to pass. If membership in these ideal communes was voluntary, if the unwilling could not be forced to join, there would always be those who preferred to live in the wretched unhappy capitalist realm beyond the circumference of the commune. Besides, what did it really matter to those who followed their bliss into the commune if others did not? It was their loss.

According to Marx and Engels, all this was nonsense. Such thinking fell under the category of utopian socialism, one of the most opprobrious epithets in the considerable lexicon of Marxist invective. In contrast to all this idle fantasizing, what Marxism offered was scientific socialism—quite a different thing altogether. But what exactly is this, and in what sense is it scientific?

The German word that is translated as *science* is *Wissenschaft*, which has a subtly different meaning from what we think of when we see the English word *science*. In German, it doesn't necessarily evoke test tubes or men in lab coats doing experiments. Rather, it implies any kind of rigorous and critical treatment of a subject. Georg Wilhelm Friedrich Hegel, who greatly influenced Marx's thinking, wrote *Science of Logic*, for example. All sorts of critical thinking could also be dubbed as "science" in German; in this sense, what was important about "science" was that it was absolutely reliable, like money in the bank—which was exactly how Marx viewed his own theory.

Socialism, according to Marx, would not come about by giddy idealists setting up their own little communes in pleasant valleys and idyllic glades. Instead, it would come all at once, in one fell swoop, to the entire society. It would represent not the isolated experimentation of romantic dreamers but an entirely new stage of history—not local but global. Furthermore, it was not a future that could be rushed or avoided. There was nothing voluntary about it; you could not make it happen if the time was not ripe, nor could you opt out of it when the time came. It was destined to occur, and occur exactly when historical conditions demanded it. You could try to resist it, as the capitalist class would certainly attempt to do, but you and they were certain to go down to defeat in the violent revolution that would end with the triumph of the proletariat—aka the working class.

To understand the logic behind these bold conclusions, we must first look at Marx's treatment of capitalism. For the utopian socialists, capitalism was simply a bad thing: the nightmare from which they were trying to awaken, the point at which history had made a terribly wrong turn. Marx rejected this approach; his theory was an adaption of Hegel's dialectical method. Far from wishing that capitalism had never happened, Marx argued that it was only due to the development of capitalism that a genuine socialist order was made possible. Prior to capitalism, any attempt to achieve economic equality would not be a sharing of wealth but a sharing of poverty. It was capitalism that provided the incentive to develop new technologies, especially labor-saving ones, and it was capitalism that rationalized the way in which labor can be organized for optimal output.

Though Marx often mocked Adam Smith, he could hardly have improved on the opening chapters of *The Wealth of Nations*, where Smith points out how a set of workers are much more productive when, instead of each one fashioning a single pin for himself, they divide up the various tasks that go into making a pin—the famous division of labor that enormously multiplies the productive capacity of any group that adopts it. In addition, the capitalist who sets up such factories is driven by his competitors to be constantly looking for new ways of making labor more efficient, including new tools and machines.

The utopian socialists were therefore mistaken in their visceral hatred of capitalism. This of course did not mean that Marx believed capitalism was just fine as it was. On the contrary, he wrote extensively about what he saw as the horrible consequences of an inherently brutal and exploitative system—but in this respect, he was hardly alone. The British reading public of the nineteenth century did not need to turn to the writings of Marx and Engels—whose *Conditions of the Working Class in England*, published in 1845, preceded *The Communist Manifesto* by three years—to find disturbing accounts of the misery of the poor and victimized.

During the dismal economic depression known, quite appropriately, as the Hungry Forties, there emerged a literary genre called the "Condition of England" novel, to which the Tory Benjamin Disraeli contributed in *Coningsby*, while the scarcely radical Elizabeth Gaskell penned *Mary Barton* and *North and South* to explore the problems faced by working-class men and women. Charles Dickens, the most popular novelist of that era, took on the plight of the poor in *Hard Times*. Even as late as 1889, in his novel *The Nether World*, George Gissing penned a harrowing depiction of the despair and hopelessness of the low-skilled worker who barely manages to eke out an existence just this side of starvation, while across the channel Emile Zola's *Germinal* was a heartbreaking account of a strike by French miners, undertaken in a spirit of collective determination and optimism, but ending tragically in disaster for all concerned.

Here a thought experiment might be helpful. Imagine that we had H. G. Wells's time machine, but used it to go back to the past—more precisely to the Hungry Forties. We get out of our contraption and proceed to make a series of visits to the various factories and mines that were operating at the time. What would we see? Young children chained to their workbenches, working twelve to thirteen hours a day under miserable conditions: boys pushing heavy carts of coal in subterranean darkness, through treacherous tunnels liable to frequent collapse, crushing tender bones and flesh beneath avalanches of rock; girls laboring all day in cotton mills, their young lungs continually breathing in the miasma of cotton particles that fill the air around them—even in the reasonably humane mills set up as model factories in Lowell, Massachusetts. Our tour would also need to include the horrendous conditions of those who had no jobs at all.

What response would we time travelers get from these brutalized workers if we cheerfully informed them that a century and a half later all would be well, that the capitalist system that exploited them so relentlessly would eventually prove to be an immense boon to future generations? Would any of them believe us? And even if they did, what difference could it possibly make to them? We might try our best to assure them that we had indeed seen the future, and that it worked—or at least, that it was working when we left it in our time machine. But in saying this, we are only making a play on words. We had not really seen into the future but only looked around us in the present world, their future, though of course none of them could live long enough to see it for themselves, let alone enjoy its benefits.

Despite the abundance of misery that accompanied the rise of capitalism, Marx still recognized that this was the price that had to be paid for progress, and rather than simply wanting to wish capitalism away, like the utopian socialists, he argued that it had to be allowed to fulfill its historical destiny. Instead of saying to the capitalists, "We have had enough of your idea of progress, let us now turn to socialism," Marx insisted that capitalism must continue to do its thing, until it ceases to be an engine of historical progress and becomes a hindrance to it, which brings us to the point that is often missed in popular ideas about Marxism.

The argument made in *Das Kapital* is that the capitalist system was destined to run out of fuel and break up of its own accordance. His thinking went like this: it is hardly a secret that capitalism goes through periodical crises, like that of the Hungry Forties in England, or the numerous crashes that shook up the nineteenth-century American economy at irregular intervals. Each time such a downturn occurred, the weaker companies failed while the stronger ones survived. In fact, the stronger ones would grow stronger and larger by absorbing those that failed. In turn, there were be fewer and fewer big companies that would be perpetually chasing after the same customers. In trying to undersell their competitors, these corporations would find that their own profits were diminishing. In order to survive, they would be forced to reduce the wages paid to their workers, which would create a truly vicious cycle, leading to what Marx dubbed the "immiseration of the proletariat." Finally, the point would be reached when the whole machinery of capitalism would grind to a halt, leaving in its wake massive unemployment and idle factories.

It is no wonder that the Great Depression of the 1930s was viewed by many as the fulfillment of Marx's vision of the future, and that in consequence many looked longingly to the USSR as offering the way out of the dilemma of failed capitalism. On the one hand, they saw in their own countries' long breadlines of laid-off workers, many of them possessing valuable skills as the result of long training. On the other hand, they saw huge technologically advanced factories whose wheels and gears were no longer spinning. These factories had already produced more goods than they could currently sell, so what was the point of producing an even larger stock of unsellable inventory?

Today, we are all aware that the Great Depression did not spell the end of capitalism. As we noted earlier, British Marxist David Harvey looked upon the period following the Great Depression and the Second World War as one during which capitalism was still delivering the goods. Yet the fact that capitalism is still alive and well today does not mean that it can continue forever. It is possible, of course, to protest that present-day capitalism is unfair, or inherently racist, or suffers from some other form of evil, but this kind of criticism of capitalism does not a Marxist make. Capitalism has always had its critics, and not just on the Left. There is also a long tradition of conservatives by temperament who hate capitalism for its "creative destruction" of traditional values, horrified by the future shock that seems to be its inevitable and irremediable byproduct. What has always made Marxism distinct from, and far more interesting than, other forms of socialism is that it claims that although capitalism had once been progressive, it would become an obstacle to future progress.

Although Marx slighted Adam Smith, there was one classical economic thinker whom he respected, and that was David Ricardo. A Sephardic Jew born in London who converted to Unitarianism, Ricardo challenged Smith's optimistic view of the future of capitalism. While Smith assumed that laissez-faire capitalism would lead to a world of plenty,

Ricardo demurred; his most well-known idea—the law of diminishing returns—would become the foundation of Marx's critique of capitalism.

The best way to understand Ricardo's law is to look at its original application to agriculture. A farmer bent on increasing the productivity of his fields will naturally begin by investing in his most fertile land. This investment will pay off because of the superior fertility of the land. But if he wishes to increase his productivity further, he will be forced to invest his efforts in land that is less fertile. The return from these fields will naturally be less than the return from his more fertile land. If he spends an equal amount of money trying to improve his inferior fields, the return on his investment will diminish, and it will continue to diminish as he tries to cultivate fields that are ever less fertile.

On June 11, 1811, the relatively obscure Ricardo met the well-known Thomas Malthus. They struck up a friendship and began a famous correspondence. They disagreed on many points of economic theory, but both subscribed to the iron law of wages, which doomed the vast majority of the population who must live off their wages to lives of squalid poverty and irredeemable misery. This was the complete repudiation of Adam Smith's optimistic view that the adoption of his laissez-faire economic policies would eventually increase the wealth of nations by lifting the general population out of poverty.

Two things should be noted here. First, the idea that capitalism would not lift the poor wage earners out of poverty, but might even make their plight worse, did not originate in the minds of dreamy-eyed socialists. Malthus, as we observed earlier, was a ferocious opponent of Condorcet's idea of unlimited progress, and he is normally classed as a reactionary today. Ricardo did not entertain any utopian schemes for improving the human lot, but believed he had simply made a brutally realistic assessment of the insurmountable limits to economic growth. Their pessimism was founded, they believed, on immutable laws of human nature.

The second point deserving of attention is why Karl Marx was drawn to the pessimism of David Ricardo in the first place. His own theory of dialectical materialism, as we have seen, articulated a gloriously optimistic view of man's future, conjuring up a world in which the poverty and misery of the masses would be completely eliminated. The solution to this puzzle is that Marx wore two different hats. His critique of capitalism was simply a more emphatic restatement of the law of diminishing returns—applying to all industries, not merely farmers. All would first begin investing in those areas of commerce and industry that gave them the greatest return on their investment, and then, like farmers, they would be forced to invest in increasingly less profitable ventures as they sought new fields of enterprise.

Moreover, their profit margin would be further reduced due to competition, which in turn would force them to cut their workers' wages. So, while Malthus and Ricardo believed that wage earners would be subject to cycles of higher wages followed by lower wages, and vice versa, Marx held that wage earners under capitalism faced the prospect of increasing immiseration that would finally terminate in the collapse of the capitalist system altogether. In other words, had Marx worn only the hat of critic of capitalism, his economic theory would rank as the most pessimistic ever conceived, far outstripping the theories of Malthus and Ricardo in gloom and doom. So how did we get to the Workers' Paradise from here?

Marx's other hat was the Phrygian cap that became a popular fashion, especially among the Jacobins during the French Revolution, but was also worn by American patriots during their War of Independence. When Marx donned this hat, he saw gleaming visions of the end of history. At first glance, it might well appear as if he was suffering from a kind of philosophical schizophrenia, but this was not the case. At the end of the tunnel of increasing poverty and misery caused by capitalism as it entered its death throes, he saw the bright light of a violent revolution, of whole nations in flames as the workers of the world rose up to overthrow their capitalist oppressors and establish the next stage of history: the era of global socialism.

There is more than a bit of sophistic legerdemain in Marx's theory of a worldwide revolution. How do you get the rabbit of socialism to jump out of the hat of moribund capitalism? This was not only a problem for Marx but for all those latter-day Marxists who argue, as David Harvey does, that at some point the limits of growth will eventually bring capitalism to its knees. It is easy to imagine a variety of quite pessimistic scenarios about what would happen if capitalism failed. Instead of leading to the next stage of history, such a failure might as easily take mankind back to an earlier era, perhaps even as far back as a hunter-gatherer society, or even a return to the law of the jungle, in which brutal gangs fight over the surviving spoils. The collapse of the USSR did not lead to a free market, as many liberal economists had assumed, but to the rise of gangster oligarchs; might not an analogous collapse of capitalism have the same results? There are a number of dystopian science fiction novels and movies in which the wealthy live in isolated enclaves, even in outer space, while the mass of the human race lives wretchedly in a state of bare subsistence. Among the most popular of such works, the *Hunger Games* series is predicated on this bleak vision of the future.

This is the first of the serious flaws in orthodox Marxism. A violent revolution might be necessary, as Marx argued, to overthrow dying capitalism, but such violent revolutions have the pernicious habit of turning on their own, making violence and terror a permanent feature of the "new order," and almost invariably end in the rise of a dictator.

Conservative critics of Marxism have, for good reasons, made this a central theme of their attack, contending that those regimes that were set up under the banner of Marxism have all proven to be disasters. There is certainly a general consensus on this question with respect to the Soviet Union and its satellites in Eastern Europe. The collapse of the USSR is a very big fact that is hard to explain away. But what about China? It has witnessed astonishing economic growth during the past several decades, during which time huge posters of Marx and Engels decorated Tiananmen Square, along with the obligatory portraits of a smiling Mao. Yet most of this growth came about only after Communist China abandoned its rigidly socialist principles and adopted many aspects of the free market. Today, China has many billionaires who may possibly think of themselves as good

Marxists, though it is questionable whether Marx would have agreed with them on this point.

Second, critics of Marxism point out that the capitalist system did not collapse at the end of the nineteenth century, nor even at the end of the twentieth century, and that it is still functioning quite well. Marx's prediction that capitalism would eventually fail has therefore been disproved. Needless to say, any self-respecting authentic Marxist today, like David Harvey, must recognize this fact, but he has a rejoinder: true, capitalism is still operating for now, and perhaps for the near future, but the day will finally come when it will inevitably collapse due to its own internal contradictions. This rejoinder, by appealing to the future, cannot be refuted by an appeal to the past or present. The beauty of any prediction is that if you make it far enough into the future, after you and everyone you know is dead, you will never need to worry about being proved wrong. Still, this is an argument that should not be dismissed too cavalierly, for reasons that we have examined throughout this book, namely that the future has surprised us many times before, and it may well surprise us again. Yet, as we have just pointed out, these socialists might be absolutely right about the eventual collapse of the capitalist system, but totally wrong about the social and historical consequences that will follow from it. In place of the utopia that they long for, they might just as easily find a dystopia of their worst nightmares.

Is anyone willing to bet that the capitalism of the present day represents the final stage of history? Such a claim surely smacks of more than a bit of the hubris that has doomed so many confident predictions about the future. Joseph Schumpeter, the Austrian economist who was an advocate of the free market, found one aspect of Marxism admirable: the recognition that capitalism was not a static system, immune to history, but was highly dynamic, changing its nature through the logic of its own internal development. In nineteenth-century America, for example, there were literally hundreds of small oil refining companies serving their local communities, but these were all doomed to perish when John D. Rockefeller's

Standard Oil began its aggressive policy of absorbing them by ruthlessly undercutting their prices.

This was made possible by the sound capitalist principle known as "economy of scale": a large company, due to its size, can afford to offer products more cheaply than a small company. The result was a radical transformation of American life, whereby small companies disappeared and giant monopolies took their place—an example of the "creative destruction" Schumpeter saw as the essence of the capitalist system. Curiously, American progressives fought tooth and nail against this process, without much success, while orthodox Marxists applauded it, regarding it as the inevitable rationalization of economic life that dialectically advanced mankind toward socialism.

Of late, a similar transformation of capitalism can clearly be seen in the advent of what is called "globalization." On the one hand, this represents a further rationalization of the economic process, while fully embracing the principle of free trade that was one of the cardinal reforms urged by Adam Smith and other advocates of the free market in the last two centuries. Generally speaking, this trend is supported by today's progressives, though this is an obvious reversal of the position taken by their predecessors at the beginning of the twentieth century, who abhorred the formation of gigantic corporations, and who presumably have looked on the multinational behemoths of today with absolute horror.

On the other hand, the current opponents of globalization are mostly those who call themselves conservatives, and who fear the increasing concentration of economic power as a threat to both the autonomy of the nation-state and to human freedom and flourishing in general. The original theory of free trade assumed that economic competition among nations would be carried out by individuals managing their own small and independent firms; it did not take into account a world in which a gargantuan state-managed economy, like that of China, could play a role equivalent to Rockefeller's Standard Oil, using its immense resources to engage in cutthroat competition against private corporations around the world that lack the backing of their respective states.

Much of our current speculation about the future is a debate between those who believe that globalization is good and inevitable, and those who believe that it is bad and doomed to failure in the long run. But it is of course also possible to believe that it is both inevitable and bad, leading to a world in which a global elite imposes its dictates on the rest of mankind, fully convinced that it knows what is best for the human race and the planet—perhaps even disguising this power grab under the nominal banner of socialism. Such an outcome might not have surprised Joseph Schumpeter, who believed that socialism of some sort would in fact win out, but for political rather than economic reasons. He did not regard this as a desirable outcome by any means, and his position on the question is highly unusual. Proponents of capitalism, unlike Schumpeter, normally see it as an economic system that will triumph in the end, while advocates of socialism, unlike Schumpeter, uniformly see socialism as a boon for mankind. To view socialism both as the wave of the future and as a setback for the human race is a heresy to both camps, but it might be that is what the future has in store for us given the current appeal of what might be called woke socialism, so fashionable among the global One Percent.

Of the various forms of socialism that we have surveyed, where does woke socialism fit in? Is it a revival of utopian socialism? Is it Marxist, as many conservatives claim? Or is it something utterly new? Indeed, is it really socialism at all? There is a tendency among some American conservatives to regard all forms of socialism as Marxist. As we have seen, this is simply not the case. Utopian socialists, as Marx and Engel dubbed them, preceded Marxism and continued to have an appeal quite independent of it. There are communes today in the United States that are throwbacks to the age of Brook Farm and Fruitlands, some no more successful than these, others proving more durable. None of them aspire to achieve control over their society's means of production and distribution. Many of them reject the inroads of modern technology, whereas orthodox Marxism always looked upon technological advances as beneficial to mankind. Indeed, a central tenet of Marxism is that the technological progress of the future will one day demand a transition from capitalism to socialism.

If the woke socialists of today merely wanted to gather in a commune where they could create a tiny fellowship where their ideals of social justice and equity prevailed, who could object to such a pursuit? But woke socialism aspires to far more than that—indeed, to be nothing less than a total transformation of society, and in this respect, it is no less ambitious than Marxism. Yet that fact alone does not make it Marxist. When trying to tie the woke movement to Marxism, critical race theory is most often offered as prima facie evidence of this connection.

Let us, however, take a look at the case made by these conservative opponents of critical race theory. Their argument goes like this: Karl Marx regarded human history as driven by the conflict between economic classes. Critical race theory also holds that human history is driven by a conflict: not between classes but between races. Both accept conflict as basic to human history, the only difference being that in CRT, race has replaced class as the source of this conflict. Ergo, CRT is Marxist, or, at the very least, inspired by Marxism. This is an egregious piece of sophistry, but one which, once we have unraveled it, will provide us with the real reason for Marx's failure to predict the future.

The conservative argument rests on one unquestioned assumption, namely that Karl Marx was the first to notice that conflict is endemic to history. In fact, it is difficult to find even a page of history that is without serious conflict of some sort—Hegel's blank pages alone being without it. In many instances, these conflicts occurred between different economic classes, like the struggle between the patricians and the plebs that would eventually lead to the breakdown of the old Roman Republic. With the exception of Sparta, the conflict between different economic class was a chronic malady of the Greek city-states, often ending in the kind of violent and bloody struggle that Thucydides describes on the island of Corcyra. Marx was the first to attempt to cast all conflict as the struggle between rival socioeconomic groups, but he was hardly singular in noting that conflict was a central theme of human history.

During Marx's own lifetime, a rival theory of conflict emerged, called social Darwinism. One variation of social Darwinism held that the central conflict in human history did not occur between different economic classes but between different races. Those who espoused this variant of social Darwinism in the past, especially in the form of Nazi "racial science," had no doubt that they were themselves the superior or master race, while other races could be charted as descending in an orderly fashion down to whichever they happened to deem the most inferior. This is certainly not the position taken by the critical race theory of today, and it would be absurd to dub it Nazism, but it is no less absurd to call it Marxism. Replacing economic class with race may give you a theory, but it will be a variation of social Darwinism—and no theory of history can be more anti-thetical to the ideas of Karl Marx.

Indeed, the most serious failure of Marxist theory is precisely its ada-mant refusal to recognize that there are many sources of conflict among human beings other than between economic classes. The British Marxist historians of the twentieth century wasted their considerable scholarship in attempting to show that the English Civil War of the seventeenth cen-tury was nothing more than a dispute between two rival economic groups, wholly ignoring the role played by the religious upheaval of the times—a factor that led earlier historians of the period to dub the English Civil War as the "Puritan Revolution." This is a prime example of modern histori-ans who misread the past due to their inability to comprehend how any-one could be motivated by something other than what motivates them. To these historians, men and women whose chief worry was where they would spend eternity are as alien as Martians.

The Marxist doctrine that bitter and violent human conflict could only arise between two rival socioeconomic classes led to a dangerous and naïve blindness to the sad fact that human beings throughout history had managed to come up with a host of completely different reasons for hating each other's guts. The tribe that dwells across the river talks funny and eats funny things; that is why we must kill and eat them. My prophet says that those who follow your prophet must be either converted or beheaded. Your theology has subtle flaws but mine does not; I must burn you at the stake. My nation needs to expand, and where better than into your nation, with its silly customs and foolish people? My race deserves to rule the world; therefore, we must enslave or exterminate those races less fit than ours.

On May 10, 1849, there was even a riot at the former Astor Place Opera House, which left between twenty-two and thirty-one rioters dead, with over a hundred injured. The cause? It was a dispute over which of two current Shakespearean actors was the better, the American Edwin Forrest or the British William Macready, with national and ethnic feelings playing their usual nefarious role in stoking animosities.

Human beings have never been at a loss to devise new and ingenious reasons to hate their fellow humans. But for Marx and Engels, this was merely an illusion. Behind all such mutual hatreds there could be only one factor: the division between those who possess wealth and those who do not. This is why, toward the end of his life, Marx was troubled and confounded by the fact that despite having the same oppressor, namely the English capitalist class, British workers and Irish workers did not join arms in a fraternal embrace but instead bitterly despised one another.

Nowhere do we see a clearer instance of Marx's blind spot than the prediction he made of what would occur in the aftermath of the American Civil War. A keen champion of the Union cause, Marx followed this huge struggle very closely, and during his stint as a correspondent for the *New York Herald Tribune*, he wrote a series of pieces on its wider historical significance. Yet Marx believed that once the capitalist ruling class—the former slave-holders—had been overthrown, the freed blacks and the poor whites would instantly rush into each other's arms, their common enemy having finally been laid low. Marx's refusal to see race as a potential source of conflict led him to think that the period of Reconstruction in the defeated South would be free of racial animosity, when in fact the legacy of this period would generate an even greater degree of racial hostility on the part of whites toward blacks. Even Kevin Anderson, one of the leading Marxists of our own day, has noted, with considerable understatement, that "Marx's dream of cross-racial solidarity was not achieved" after the Civil War, as new laws were put in force throughout the South prohibiting free blacks who were highly skilled in various trades from competing against whites.

Marx might have learned something from this failed prediction, but his theory precluded it. Ideology trumped mere brute fact, as so often happens. Instead of revising his ideas, he came up with a method of explaining why ordinary human beings refused to act in accordance with his theory. This is the Marxist doctrine of "false consciousness," one of the first revisions of his original theory. An individual acted with true consciousness when he identified himself in his correct relationship to the means of production and distribution. If you worked in a factory, you identified as a member of the proletariat, and nothing else really counted as part of your essential identity—if you were a man or woman; yellow, black, red, brown, or white; English, German, or Chinese; tall or short; handsome or hideous; Jew, Muslim, Christian, or Buddhist. If you regarded yourself as anything other than a member of the proletariat, first, last, and always, then you were the sad victim of false consciousness.

For Marx, such false consciousness was not the result of any spontaneous tendency of different ethnic or racial groups to hate each other, but of a deliberate strategy on the part of the ruling class. Since the oppressed classes always outnumbered the ruling class, if they were to unite, as Marx and Engels urged them to do, their vastly greater numbers would easily overmatch the much smaller ruling class and its hired flunkeys. In consequence of this demographic fact, the ruling class fiendishly resorted to the age-old method of divide and conquer. By turning members of the working class against one another, based on ethnic or racial differences, they could achieve their objective of distracting the workers from their real enemy—their capitalist masters—while turning them against those who should be their allies in the class struggle.

The doctrine of false consciousness, although it solved Marx's problem of the failure of the working class to unite, completely undermined one of the main selling points of Marxism: its claim to scientific objectivity. When English astronomer Edmond Halley predicted the reappearance of the comet that came to bear his name, he became famous, but the comet would have returned at the exact same time even if he had never made his calculations. If the predictions of Marx and Engels were scientific in the same sense, then it would not matter if Marx and Engels had ever lived—capitalism was predestined to collapse and socialism to take its place, just as Halley's comet would return on schedule, even if Halley had never lived. Scientific laws, of both astronomy and history, operate independently of their discoverers.

The moment, however, that the doctrine of false consciousness was thrown into the mix of Marxist thought, all of its claims of being a scientific theory, yielding infallible predictions about the future, went down the drain. If the proletariat had to be educated and trained for its historical mission of overthrowing the capitalist system, then there was nothing inevitable about the collapse of capitalism or the advent of socialism. Halley's comet did not need to "have its conscious raised" in order to show up on time. If the revolution could only come about through the indoctrination of the workers in the theory of Marxism, then the theory refuted itself, since it now required the active intervention by Marxists to bring about what was previously assumed to be historically inevitable. The socialist future could no longer be counted upon to come automatically. Instead, it had to be worked, shaped, and guided by human hands and hearts. This turned Marxism from a scientific theory into a political program like any other—one which demanded that workers completely reject their ethnic, religious, racial, and national identities, and join hands together as fellow workers of the world.

Once this is understood, it is easy to see how Marx would regard the identity politics of our time. A Marxist critique of critical race theory might begin by noting how suspiciously popular it is among today's ruling elite, endorsed and championed by some of the world's largest and most powerful corporations. Critical race theory claims to be interested in achieving the vaguely defined but clearly utopian goal of "social justice," but that is mere window dressing to deceive the credulous. Its real purpose is to turn the members of working class against one other, on the basis of race. Although CRT does not employ the crude racism that the post-Civil-War

Southern Bourbon Democrats used to stoke hostility between poor blacks and poor whites, it happily exploits racial grievances for the purpose of distracting both whites and blacks from confronting their real oppressors: the elite capitalist class. CRT is revealed to be simply the latest tool by which the masses can be manipulated into hating each other instead of their capitalist masters. What a brilliant touch, to dress up this new method of divide and conquer as a form of Marxism!

The fashionable "identity politics" of today encourages people to define themselves by race, ethnicity, sexual preference, religion, and gender (a multitude of possible genders at that). In this smorgasbord of different identities, to which new dishes are added almost every day, there is one dish that is oddly missing: class consciousness. Instead of railing against the privilege of wealth and capital, the liberal media stars, who normally have plenty of both, aim their denunciation at an abstraction called "white privilege," despite the fact that between 40 and 50 percent of non-Hispanic whites are solidly in the working class, and even despite the fact that in the USA there are currently 40 million more white Americans living in poverty than black Americans. In fact, it is hard to avoid drawing the conclusion, even if you are not a Marxist, that identity politics deliberately aims to subvert any sense of solidarity among the American working class by turning its members against each other, with the top one percent of the richest Americans telling ordinary Americans of one color that their true enemies are ordinary Americans of another.

To Marx, this proliferation of different identities, none of them based on class, would seem like false consciousness run amok. Yet the very fact that, at the end of the first quarter of the twenty-first century, we are mincing our core sense of identity into ever smaller units, encouraged and championed by those on the Left but not those on the Right, would suggest that orthodox Marxism is as dead a doornail, especially among woke progressives. But in fact, orthodox Marxism died over a century ago, on the eve of the Great War.

Perhaps it was true, as Marx argued, that the devious capitalist masters could easily manipulate those pesky Irish and English workers, or the poor and often barely literate white dirt-farmers of the Old South—none overly educated people, to be sure. But what about the members of those European political parties who steeped themselves in Marxist doctrine, namely the Socialist parties of the advanced European nations on the eve of the Great War? All had surely read *The Communist Manifesto*, and many had mastered the daunting complexities of *Das Kapital*. Surely here, if anywhere, was the place to find devout, one might even say "highly trained" Marxists, who would certainly never be duped into turning against their proletariat brothers.

When all hell broke loose in August of 1914 and the Great War was about to sweep across Europe, what did these Marxist parties do? The German Socialist Party, the largest Marxist organization in the world, voted the German government the war credits necessary to defeat their enemy, with only a handful of holdouts. So too did the French Marxists, again with only a few abstentions. Yet who among them did not recall the famously rousing lines with which *The Communist Manifesto* had ended: "Workers of the world, unite. You have nothing to lose but your chains. You have a world to win." In the catastrophe that later become known as the First World War, the workers of the world divided into mutually hostile national camps, and poured into the trenches intent on maiming and killing their fellow workers of the world. Orthodox Marxism, like many other visions of the future, had failed, as so many other hopeful visions of the future had failed, and would fail again, by refusing to acknowledge the persistent perversity of human nature.

Yet this debacle of orthodox Marxism did not result in the death of Marxism, as the advent of the Bolshevik regime three years after the start of the war demonstrates. After the outbreak of the First World War, dedicated Marxists like Vladmir Lenin were forced to come to terms with the failure of the European working class to rally altogether against the war. In his book *Imperialism, The Highest Stage of Capitalism*, published in 1917, Lenin argued that the war currently raging had been caused by the conflict between the competing imperial aspirations of the major European nations. This was certainly a questionable assumption, but the most striking and original idea presented in his book was pregnant with immense historical consequences.

Orthodox Marxism had always assumed that the revolution would naturally come about in the most advanced capitalist nations, whose working classes, enlightened by Marxist theory, would be in the vanguard of the revolutionary movement. This had not happened. Worse, the European working class had volunteered to fight their brothers in the great imperialist war.

To minds less committed than Lenin's, this should have been the death knell of Marxism. If great conflicts could arise out of factors such as nationalism, ethnic divisions, racial animosity, or religious bigotry, then the Marxist model for predicting the future was untenable, because it assumed that only a single factor, class conflict, governed the historical process. But if an array of other factors was capable of shaping history, then Marx's oversimplified model broke down—the usual fate of all overly simplified models, since a model is only reliable if it includes all the variables that can affect the predicted outcome, and Marx's did not.

Lenin, however, did not give up. Instead, he proposed turning Marx's theory upside down. Marx had believed the socialist revolution would be initiated by the working class of the advanced capitalist nations, and only after that had come about would liberation come to the more backward nations. Lenin reversed this scenario. The revolution was now expected to come first in the backward nations and among the oppressed people of the imperialist powers, and only then would it spread to the advanced nations and their working classes.

This was obviously no minor revision of Marxism but an entirely new theory, out of which came the distinctive ideology of Leninism. No doubt Lenin believed in his new doctrine, yet it is hard not to suspect that there was an element of opportunism in his radical inversion of orthodox Marxism. Russia was clearly not one of the advanced capitalist nations. It was overwhelmingly a land of peasants, who constituted 85 percent of its population, with only a small proletariat, compared to England, France, or Germany. If Russian Marxists remained true to orthodoxy, they would need to wait until these more advanced nations had achieved their own socialist revolutions before they could even begin to hope for a similar transformation of their own land.

Lenin, however, was not a patient man. Having witnessed the abysmal failure of the socialist parties of Germany and France to unite against the war, he decided that it was his mission to start the worldwide revolution in his own very backward country of Czarist Russia. When, against all odds, Lenin and his Bolshevik party seized power in 1917, he confidently expected that the war-torn nations of Europe would quickly follow the Soviet lead. In defeated Germany, there was in fact an effort to seize power by Communists, led by Karl Liebknecht and Rosa Luxemburg—two of the German socialists who had originally opposed the war. The so-called Spartacist uprising began on January 5, 1919, but it lasted only a week. It was brutally put down and its leaders assassinated. The Communist revolution in Hungary also suffered the same fate, and Lenin's hope of a Europe-wide revolution collapsed.

Now what? The most obvious problem was how to apply Marx's theory, which concerned itself with the conflict between the proletariat and the capitalist class, to an immense land that was overwhelmingly dominated by peasants. Karl Marx had never seen even a glint of revolutionary potential in a class that was submerged in what he dismissively called "the idiocy of rural life."

It is true that the Bolsheviks, in their seizure of power, had the support of the peasants, but this was only due to their shrewd but specious promise to permit the Russian peasants to own the land that they had heretofore labored on as tenants. Giving peasants their own land may have been just, but it hardly constituted the kind of progress the new Soviet republic would have to make if it were to catch up with the advanced industrial societies of Europe and North America. In fact, giving peasants a reason to stay on the land, instead of moving into the cities where they could work in factories, was a step backward, however politically expedient.

When faced with the problem of how to turn the peasants of the USSR into a revolutionary force, Lenin hit upon an idea that would have momentous consequences. Normally, the peasant class had been looked upon as a homogenous and undifferentiated mass—one peasant was very much like another. Not so, Lenin argued, pointing out, quite correctly, that some peasants were marginally better off than others. How had these peasants come to have more? Common sense might suggest that perhaps they worked harder or drank less, or were thriftier, or perhaps had fewer children than the poorer ones. It might be that some were just luckier than others—their cows happened to have more calves. Lenin brushed aside all these factors and came up with his own answer: the reason some peasants were relatively well off was because they *exploited* the poorer peasants.

The concept of exploitation was an essential part of orthodox Marxism, where it had a precise technical meaning. The capitalist class exploited the working class whenever it paid them less than what they produced. Here is a simple example: John owns a factory where George and Robert make ten widgets a day each. John pays them a dollar for each widget, which he then turns around and sells for two dollars. Of course, John has to pay for overhead expenses, and it turns out that after subtracting these costs, he makes a dollar and twenty-five cents per widget. The twenty-five cents goes into his pocket as profit, which he may spend on himself or reinvest in his factory. He would not be exploiting George and Robert if he gave them the twenty-five cents instead, but then he would not be making a profit, and George and Robert would soon be looking for a new job where the boss was not such an idiot. In fairness to Marx, he believed such exploitation was dialectically necessary in order for capitalism to create the modern industrial world. The exploitation of labor was the only means by which a surplus of capital could be achieved, a preliminary step toward creating a more prosperous world.

Whatever one might think of Marx's concept of exploitation, it only makes sense in the context in which it was originally applied: the relationship between capitalists and those who work for them. But the well-off peasants were most emphatically not members of the capitalist class. True, some peasants might hire others to do some of the work, but this was only incidental to the economic life of the peasantry. Likewise, the rich peasants might loan money to the poorer ones, and even charge an exorbitant rate of interest, but this petty financial activity did not make the better-off peasants into capitalists.

Lenin's ingenious and disingenuous application of Marx's theory of class conflict to the rural peasantry would later be adopted by both Stalin in the USSR in his campaign against the Kulaks, the new class villains (i.e., better-off peasants), and by Mao Zedong in his campaign against the Chinese peasants who had the bad luck to be slightly more prosperous than average. Whatever animosity might have previously existed between the two groups of peasants was deliberately stirred into a fury, with a loss of human lives that must be calculated in the millions.

The Italian Marxist Antonio Gramsci was also faced with the challenge of explaining the failure of orthodox Marxism to prevent the Great War. He did this by elaborating on the concept of false consciousness. Previously, false consciousness was a condition of certain individuals or even groups. Gramsci, however, elevated it to an entire theory of how culture works. The dominant class always has a set of self-serving values. No ruling elite, after all, has ever believed that it didn't deserve to rule, either by its willingness to defy death in a warrior society, or its noble bloodline in traditional aristocracies, or by its intellectual superiority, as in ancient China and modern meritocracies. Once this uncritical self-confidence vanishes, the days of elite rule are numbered.

Gramsci's most famous concept, cultural hegemony, describes a condition in which the non-elite classes of a society have come to accept the rule of the elite as natural and even obvious. Despite being oppressed by the elite, the other classes simply cannot imagine any other social order than the one under which they live, nor could their ancestors. The challenge for Gramsci was how to get the masses to recognize that they were oppressed and, even more critically, how to get them to commit themselves to the struggle to liberate themselves from the cultural hegemony that continued to hold them spellbound.

The concept of cultural Marxism owes its origin to Gramsci, but it misses an essential point in his theory. Today's conservative intellectuals, who see self-proclaimed progressives dominating our major cultural institutions—academia, news media, even many churches—have supposed them to be carrying out Gramsci's game plan. The "march through the institutions," as these conservatives call it, is exactly the campaign to gain cultural hegemony as prescribed by Gramsci—in effect, a cultural coup engineered by progressive intellectuals. The phrase "long march through the institutions," however, did not come from Gramsci but from Rudi Dutschke, who coined it in 1967, with clear reference to Mao's celebrated Long March that took place between 1934 and 1935. None of Dutschke's writings even refer to Gramsci. What had excited Dutschke was Mao's Cultural Revolution, which was not a march, but a violent rampage through Chinese institutions in which academics of all kinds were systematically humiliated, degraded, and sometimes even murdered by their former students.

Furthermore, even Dutschke himself did not aim to infiltrate the old institutions but rather to create new ones. Herbert Marcuse, influenced by Dutschke, argued that socialists needed to learn the technical skills and knowledge offered by the established institutions: "how to program and read computers, how to teach at all levels of education, how to use the mass media, how to organize production…how to design." Once the socialists have acquired these practical skill sets, they would then be in a position to make "the concerted effort to build up *counterinstitutions*." [Emphasis mine.]

For Marcuse and Dutschke, socialists needed to create their own institutions, outside of the established ones. They could and should learn the useful tricks and practices at these establishments, but they never dreamed of reforming them from within. How do you radicalize an established institution, deeply set in its ways and its routines, with those who benefit from its perks always willing to obstruct and hinder any serious effort at institutional reform, not to mention outright revolution? For this reason, these socialists wanted their own schools and universities, their own newspapers and TV channels, holding out not the least hope that the institutions that stood for the status quo could ever to be redeemed from their innate tendency to look after their own narrow self-interest. They were especially distrustful of the academic intellectual, too often grossly out of touch with any practical experience of the world—exactly the kind of intellectuals, in short, for whom Gramsci had no use:

"The traditional and vulgarized type of the intellectual is given by the man of letters, the philosopher, and the artist. Therefore, journalists, who claim to be men of letters, philosophers, artists, also regard themselves as the 'true' intellectuals. In the modern world, technical education, closely bound to industrial labor, even at the most primitive and unqualified level, must form the basis of the new type of intellectual."

How many of today's progressive intellectuals fit Gramsci's ideal? How many have received a good technical education or have had a hands-on involvement with industrial labor? Virtually none. They are proudly out of touch with the practical concerns and anxieties of the average working man and woman, turning up their noses at their values. The celebrated march through the institutions never happened. The institutions never ceased to be defenders of the powers that be. That is what they are there for. It just so happens that today, the powers that be have a new agenda. The socialists of an earlier time, such as Gramsci, Dutschke, and Marcuse, would have been bewildered to find established universities and media conglomerates marching forward hand in hand with tech billionaires and the world's meta-corporations, claiming to be the vanguard of a new socialism that has no use for the working class, whose values they despise and whose current populist revolt in both the USA and Europe they are doing their best to crush.

The history of socialism, however, is rich in such ironies. For example, it is quite possible that Marxism had considerably more influence on the defenders of the capitalist status quo than it did on the proletariat. Utopian socialism, after all, could never be a threat to capitalism, any more than the woke socialism of our day. No danger was posed by mere enclaves of lotus-eating dropouts who had no desire to meddle with the capitalist system and who, indeed, were trying to remove themselves as far from it as they could. Marxism, on the other hand, aimed at nothing less than overthrowing world capitalism. Here was a threat that made the capitalists sit up and take notice.

Otto von Bismarck, astute politician that he was, took the threat seriously and decided that the best defense against it was to ameliorate the condition of the working class. The better off they were, the less likely they would be to revolt. Hence, in 1889, he inaugurated the first welfare system, eventually granting German workers health insurance and unemployment benefits. The other capitalist nations followed his lead, especially Great Britain and France, while the United States only adopted similar measures in the wake of the Great Depression—and even then, timidly, and largely due to President Franklin D. Roosevelt's fear of economic populism from the Left, as represented by Huey Long of Louisiana.

In Germany, however, Bismarck's innovation was so effective that many German Marxists abandoned the idea that a violent overthrow of capitalism was needed, and were content with gradual improvement of the worker's lot. Eduard Bernstein, who had once been a close friend of Marx, led the way, and the socialist welfare states of Europe became embodiments of the same spirit, while those still devoted to orthodox Marxism howled at this apostasy. Those who think of the welfare state as Marxist in origin could not be more mistaken. It was seen by the old Marxists for what it was: a method of avoiding revolution, which is why they fought tooth and nail against any proposal designed to improve the lives of the working class—an attitude which ordinary working-class men and women found hard to swallow. Promises of a future Golden Age could not feed a child or warm a home today.

Here is a curious thought experiment. Imagine if Marx and Engels had in fact never been born and no one else had ever developed an analogous theory. Without the fear of a Marxist-inspired revolution, would the capitalists have seen any reason to improve the lot of the working class? Would they, out of the goodness of their heart, have provided shorter hours, safer working conditions, health care, and so forth? Or would the horrendous and bleak factory system of the nineteenth century have continued into our own time—assuming, of course, that a violent revolution did not sweep away the whole edifice of the capitalist system? In short, did Karl Marx, by scaring the hell of the capitalist class, inadvertently save capitalism from itself?

Here is another. Let us suppose that the socialist parties of France and Germany had heeded *The Communist Manifesto*'s rousing final lines and decided to unite their forces against their nations' decision to go to war. And let us further suppose that they succeeded in their effort, and that the catastrophe that was the Great War was prevented by their determined opposition. If so, would anyone today recognize the name Vladmir Lenin, aside from the few historians who specialize in obscure revolutionary movements of the early twentieth century? Or for that matter, would the names Hitler or Stalin mean anything to us today? If Italy had not been suckered into joining the Allied cause by being promised territorial rewards that never came through, it would not have spilled the blood of its men in futile campaigns against the Austrians. Mussolini might have gone on to have an interesting journalistic career, but he would never have become *Il Duce*. But such a world never came into being.

The irony here is patent. If the European working class had all behaved like good Marxists, it is quite possible that no Communist regime could ever have come to power either in Russia or the rest of the world. Indeed, after the Great War, both Lenin and Stalin stopped putting their faith in world revolution among the advanced nations, such as Germany and England, recognizing that regimes like their own had only to come power as the result of anarchy brought on by war. It was only because power was literally lying in the streets that the Bolsheviks had been able to pick it up.

CHAPTER NINE

TOWARD A KINDER,
GENTLER TOTALITARIANISM

"Cancel culture" is certainly a sign of our times. The progressives who promote it are, as usual, sincerely convinced that they know what is best for everyone else, and feel that their ideal of culture should prevail. Unfortunately for them, some people have other ideals that conflict with the progressive agenda. How much better it would be if these wayward elements of our culture would simply go away, recognizing that they belong in the trash bin of history. Those who "cling to their guns and religion," as Obama said put it, need to be made to see that they are on the wrong side of history. Indeed, President Obama once remarked that if he had been allowed to talk to every American citizen in their own home, he would be able to convince them that he was right. The unspoken assumption behind this flagrant bit of vanity was that his listeners would remain dutifully silenced, no doubt with awe. Apparently, it never occurred to Obama, even as a possibility, that he might learn a thing or two from his hosts by asking what they thought. But he was there to talk, not to listen. Perhaps their minds could be changed if only Obama had had the chance to have that talk of his, but barring that, a thoroughgoing program of cancel culture might do the trick.

The woke progressives of today are hardly the first advanced thinkers to believe that they should have total control over every aspect of their culture. They are not the first to seek to silence those they deem to be on the wrong side of history. Nor are they the first who wish to politicize every aspect of a society's culture, from the high arts to the education of elementary school children to public sporting events. All this has been done before. There is a word for this desire for the total control over culture: *totalitarianism*. Needless to say, the woke progressives are seeking a gentler, kinder form of totalitarianism, though none of them are about to use this term to define their objectives.

Nowadays, after all, the term *totalitarian* automatically invokes images of gulags and concentration camps, the Cheka and the Gestapo, Brownshirt thugs and SS sadists, mass murder and mass starvation—all the evils that we associate with Soviet Communism, Italian fascism, and National Socialism. For those who championed these regimes, however, the term stood for a utopian ideal, in the pursuit of which millions of men and women dedicated, and often sacrificed, their lives. The Nazis' confidence in their glowing future was poignantly captured in the musical *Cabaret*, when at the outdoor biergarten a blonde Nazi youth stands up and, with the deepest sincerity—a sincerity that disturbs us even while we are moved by it—sings, "Tomorrow belongs to me." It didn't; the poor kid probably died along with countless others of his generation in the bloody fields of the Eastern Front. The great conflicts of the previous century took place between forces which all claimed that tomorrow belonged to them. Faced with the ambition of today's woke progressives to impose total control over our cultural life, perhaps it is time to re-examine the origins of totalitarianism.

The Italian philosopher Benedetto Croce, a longtime critic of Mussolini's regime, argued that the seeds of fascism had been planted by an earlier artistic movement that had been launched in Milan in 1909 with the publication by the poet Filippo Tommaso Marinetti of his "Manifesto of Futurism." Its creed embraced a host of causes, all of which were seen as progress. The futurists abhorred the past and wanted no part of it. They celebrated violence, youth, speed, and technology in all its many manifestations: the airplane, the car, the factory, and whatever else was new. Originality became an end in itself, and shocking old-fashioned bourgeoise tastes a sufficiently worthy goal of futuristic artists.

Italian fascism was "futuristic" in the sense that it offered a radical break with both liberalism and parliamentary democracy, but it also represented a radical break with the traditional forms of dictatorship. Normally, a dictator was simply concerned with obtaining and holding on to power by any means necessary. The power such dictators held could be used to enrich themselves and their cronies at the expense of the rest of their society, the typical pattern of virtually all petty dictators who ever lived. The conventional dictator required from his subjects only passive acquiescence to his rule and, like Machiavelli's Prince, if he could not be loved, he was content to be feared. He regarded his subjects merely as sheep to be fleeced, often with complete disregard to their future prospects and the welfare of society in general.

It was another critic of Mussolini who came up with a term to distinguish the new fascist regime from petty dictatorships, past and present. In 1923, the Italian politician Giovanni Amendola coined the word *totalitario* as a way of indicating what was novel about the fascist regime: its determination to control and shape the entire social order according to its own ideals and ideology. Mussolini, who had previously been a socialist journalist, did not seek power to further his purely private ends but to create a new Italy. While the typical dictator merely desires to enrich himself at the expense of the status quo, Mussolini embarked on a grand project of reconstructing society from top to bottom. For Amendola, it was precisely this grandiose ambition to reshape society in its totality that made Italian fascism more dangerous than an ordinary dictatorship—a thesis that was tragically vindicated when Amendola became one of the earliest victims of the new regime. In July 1925, he was severely beaten by fifteen fascist Blackshirts wielding clubs, and died from his ordeal the following year.

The very concept of *totalitario* might well have died with Amendola, but it was audaciously revived by the leading Italian philosopher of fascism,

Giovanni Gentile, who agreed with Amendola that Italian fascism was entirely distinct from past dictatorships, for exactly the same reasons that Amendola had advanced. The Italian fascists' goal *was* a compete reorganization of the entire social order in accordance with their own ideals. For Gentile, unlike Amendola, this totalizing impulse was not seen as a menace to be feared but as the sole path to national salvation. Mussolini himself also embraced *totalitario* as a way of characterizing his own political ideals. He wanted to use the apparatus of the state to lay the foundations of a future community in which its members would be totally and unanimously devoted to the ethos of his own fascist party. The party had not created the state, but it had successfully transformed it into an instrument to advance the fascist vision of the future: a revitalized Italy, once again a great nation, that would be based on a revival of the tough ethos of ancient Rome, symbolized by the *fasces*, a bundle of rods with a projecting axe blade that the Roman lictor carried with him as a not-so-subtle reminder of the ultimate source of authority—hence the term *fascist*.

Despite the origin of the term in the Italian fascist movement, it has long been the practice to group Soviet Communism, Nazism, and Italian fascism under the label *totalitarian*. Today, the word has acquired an array of connotations arising from how these three different regimes operated in practice, during the period in which they held power. But as its original usage indicates, it was first used not to describe an existing system but an ideal to be realized in the future. When Mussolini's admirer Adolf Hitler spoke about his own vision of the new German Reich, he invariably presented it as a goal that would require many future generations to achieve. Stalin also recognized that the full realization of the Communist utopia would likewise demand a multigenerational struggle. As in fascist Italy, both the Third Reich and the USSR were states that had become tools of a single fanatically dedicated party, each with a different vision of the future, each utopian in its own way.

All were clearly authoritarian, yet none of them ever came remotely close to achieving Mussolini's succinct definition of totalitarianism: "Everything within the state, nothing outside the state, nothing against the state." True, Mussolini famously got the trains to run on time, but most Italians lived their normal lives without giving much thought to the state. In regimes both absolutist, like those of Europe's Enlightened despots, and totalitarian, like Mussolini's, most of life goes on *outside* the state. It was also absurd to claim that there was nothing *against* the state. If there were no forces against the state, then presumably there would no need to suppress them, no need for secret police, a Gestapo or a Cheka, or concentration camps, Gulags, torture chambers, show trials, or executions in public or carried out in dark, filthy basements.

The desire to achieve total control over every aspect of a society has long been the ideal proposed by utopian thinkers, from Plato to Charles Fourier. The so-called totalitarian regimes of the twentieth century shared this ideal, but they applied it not to relatively small communes but to entire nations. The tyrants of the ancient world, like Machiavelli's Prince, were limited in their capacity to influence the minds of their subjects. Fear was most often the chosen method of persuading others to obey, simply because there were really no more effective means. You could hire thugs to beat up your enemies, you could pay mercenaries to fight your battles, or have men of learning write your encomium, but how could you possibly convince the masses to love you?

With the advent of the means of mass communication, all of this changed. Radio was the first breakthrough, and it was exploited to the fullest by both Mussolini and Adolf Hitler to stunning effect. Everyone could now hear the voice of the leader, and newsreels permitted you to see them. Their faces and voices became as familiar as those of your closest intimates. You now felt that you knew your leader personally. In the United States, President Franklin Roosevelt pioneered the fireside chat, while Winston Churchill used his formidable eloquence to keep the British public on his side during their darkest hours. Later, television would add an even more convincing illusion of intimacy, and those who knew how best to establish a rapport with their audience inevitably had an edge on their competition.

George Orwell's novel *1984* was written after the advent of television but at a time when there were only a few TV sets, so it is perhaps forgivable that he failed to grasp its real potential as a tool of propaganda. His protagonist, Winston Smith, a member of the intelligentsia, had an enormous TV screen in his shabby apartment, but it was used to watch *him*. Presumably other members of the bureaucratic elite had their own giant monitoring screens as well. For Orwell, the threat of television was that it would be used as a means of surveillance, not as a means of propaganda. Indeed, it became the most powerful and effective tool ever devised for shaping and controlling public opinion, though it is possible that social media may give it a run for its money.

Orwell failed to see that the advent of television heralded not a new era of 24/7 surveillance but a new age of 24/7 news coverage, brought into your own home by people who decide what is newsworthy, what you need to hear. It is possible, in theory, that the news media could be used soberly and objectively, but from the beginning, the dangers of abuse were evident and rules of fairness were established, but in vain.

The early days of television news came during the 1950s, a period in American history when politics was only a small part of life, confined to its strictly delimited sphere. It was something we thought about at election time, if even then. Children of that era were advised by their parents, as my father told me, that there were two things you should never talk about with people you didn't know well: politics and religion. In retrospect, it is astonishing how many things we still had left to talk about. During the past seventy years, however, the domain of the political has expanded at an ever-accelerating pace.

Those realms of human endeavor that were once seen as above the political fray, or at least outside it, have now become thoroughly politicized. No field of study is exempt from it, especially education—from kindergarten to the most advanced academic environments. Even American pastimes like baseball or football games have ceased to be politically neutral events. There is virtually no aspect of human life that has not been politicized.

Even mathematics has become a source of political controversy, along with the other sciences, while art and literature must be politically correct to be taken seriously. Even opera, the most escapist form of all the arts, has been dragooned into carrying a political message. Gioachino Rossini's opera *Mosè in Egitto* (*Moses in Egypt*) has been retooled into a vehicle for anti-Israeli propaganda under the guidance of Graham Vick, while a recent version of Wagner's immense *Ring* cycle takes up the plight of refugees flying to Europe carrying only their luggage with them.

Make no mistake—the impulse here is totalitarian. Indeed, perhaps the best definition of that slippery concept is the desire to make everything under the sun about politics. Furthermore, when the colossal power of the modern media is taken into account, the temptation to use it to advance one's own political views becomes irresistible.

Edward Bernays, the nephew of Sigmund Freud, mainly confined his activities to new and ingenious ways of advertising commercial products. He sold Lucky Strike cigarettes to women by dubbing them feminist "Torches of Freedom." Later he promoted Dixie Cups by arguing that they were more sanitary than ordinary ones. But Bernays, busy man that he was, also found time to write a short book entitled *Propaganda*, in which he unwittingly disclosed the keys to the successful manipulation of mass opinion, which did not require state control of the media. When a single party—like the Italian fascists, the National Socialists, or the Bolsheviks—holds a monopoly over the media, propaganda efforts cannot avoid coming across as heavy-handed. Eventually such efforts are simply shrugged off as nothing more than the official party line. According to Bernays, to sell a product or a party line successfully, two things are required. First, the message must be repeated over and over, but to avoid the trap that totalitarian regimes invariably fall into, it is essential that the message appear to come from as many different sources as possible. This second requirement creates the all-important illusion that nothing is really being sold, neither product nor party line, but simply that everyone else is already buying it, so you should buy it too, be it Lucky Strikes or "gender-affirming care."

Today's mainstream media certainly make it look like they have all studied Bernays's little book. They uniformly champion all the same progressive causes, while dismissing anyone who dares to question them. Often, they do not even take the trouble of writing their own copy, but are content with parroting word for word the progressive party line du jour. To put such a potent means of persuasion into the hands of a single political interest group is to risk the advent of a "kinder, gentler" totalitarianism that has no need of gulags or concentration camps in order to bring about the desired uniformity of public opinion. There is no need to suppress dissent if you can make sure it does not occur in the first place.

It is hard to imagine how the woke movement could have caught on so suddenly without virtually uniform support from the producers and distributers of public opinion. This is especially true considering Americans' attitude toward socialism, including the "democratic" socialism favored by the woke.

In an earlier chapter, we established that the woke movement is the antithesis of orthodox Marxism. In the next chapter, we will examine whether woke socialism is socialism at all, and not merely a romantic posturing of a self-gratulatory elite.

CHAPTER TEN

THE ROAD TO WOKEDOM

American polls currently show that, in comparison with the past, a shockingly large number of voters favor something that goes by the name of Democratic Socialism. But obviously this is not your father's socialism. The tip-off here is the huge array of mega-corporations that are happy to sing woke party lines. Perhaps the big shots at these corporations are suffering from a severe bout of Marxian false consciousness, blinded to their role as the captains and beneficiaries of the capitalist system—or perhaps not. Yet this curious and unprecedented conjunction of the immensely wealthy and the woke oppressed might have a future, even a big one. It may well provide a shiny new ideological banner, allowing the rich and the powerful to disguise their bid to become even richer and more powerful.

We have already seen the dubious claims that woke socialism has to be a revival of Marxism, but now we will examine whether it even can claim to be progressive, at least in any sense that might be recognized by the progressives of the past. Quite naturally, today's progressives would rather recall those past causes that paint them in a favorable light. The abolition of slavery is by far the most conspicuous case, but there are others of more recent vintage, such as the struggle to give women the right to vote and to participate in public life, and the fight to give black Americans the same civil rights as white Americans. These were considerable battles, which took place over decades, and in the long run those causes were victorious, despite the many forces arrayed against them.

Those who championed these noble causes therefore had good reason to regard themselves as progressives. But there were many other causes that were considered progressive in their time but look quite different today. Take populism: In late nineteenth-century America, populism and progressivism went hand-in-hand. The Democratic Party nominated the progressive/populist William Jennings Bryan three times for the presidency. In the first half of the twentieth century, there was the now-defunct midwestern tradition of progressive Republicans like "Fightin' Bob" La Follette from Wisconsin. This brand of economic populism, embraced more often by Democrats and Independents, championed the little guy over big corporations and opposed our meddling in foreign affairs, producing such staunch noninterventionists as Burton Wheeler of Montana. It distrusted egghead intellectuals and their ivory towers, and deeply suspected the sinister machinations of the "Eastern Establishment." It was the party of farmers, mechanics, and artisans. Its favorite political treatise was *The Wizard of Oz*. In short, it was everything that today's progressives are not. The only thing they have in common is a name.

In fact, all the early progressives, like Ida Tarbell, were on the side of the little guy, and fulminated against the monopolistic tendencies of giant corporations, like Standard Oil. This position was perhaps most eloquently affirmed by Supreme Court Justice Louis Brandeis in his essay "The Curse of Bigness," which argued any concentration of too much power—either in the hands of government officials or private corporations—posed a grave threat to liberty and democracy. Today's woke progressives are aligned with international corporations, support globalization, and advocate for bigger and more invasive government; their creed might be called "The Blessings of Bigness." To them, the existential threat to liberty and democracies comes from the little guy, and populism is regarded as Enemy Number One.

It is the cause of eugenics, however, that provides the most startling example of a complete reversal of the progressive agenda. The Princeton historian of the subject, Thomas C. Leonard, notes that "in 1928, 378 college courses were dedicated to subject of eugenics," adding, "Hundreds, perhaps thousands of Progressive Era scholars and scientists proudly called themselves eugenicists." Furthermore, American progressives did not merely discuss eugenics as a theory but pushed through legislation that resulted in the forced sterilization of tens of thousands of Americans. New Jersey was a pioneer in this respect, and the law it passed was signed by its very progressive governor at the time, Woodrow Wilson. For many of the progressives of that era, the elimination of all people biologically unequipped for the challenging demands of modern life was a surely a step forward. Yet today, for obvious reasons, the very idea of eugenics evokes the memory of Nazi Germany and its inhuman application of the "science" of eugenics.

The prohibition of alcohol was another progressive cause. No one, then or now, could deny that the wanton abuse of alcohol takes a staggering toll on both individuals and society at large. Like the feeble-minded, the hopeless alcoholic had no role to play in the march of progress. Yet the great American experiment known as Prohibition succumbed to that bane of all would-be reformers: the law of unintended consequences. Organized crime, which had previously played only a marginal role in American society, flourished and grew to immense proportions, providing bootleg liquor to those Americans whose taste for alcohol no law had the power to quench. In due course, the great experiment was brought to an end, though the criminal organizations it had produced became a sordid fixture on the American scene.

On the other hand, looking back to earlier times, it is easy to find lonely groups of genuine progressives who promoted ideas for reforming society that have indeed come to be taken for granted by virtually everyone today. These crusaders could quite rightly claim to be ahead of their time. In the America of the nineteenth century, they championed universal manhood suffrage, abhorred slavery and wanted to see it either eliminated gradually, such as Henry Clay, or insisted on its immediate abolition, such as William Lloyd Garrison. There were the early feminists, such as the brilliant Margaret Fuller, who embraced then-radical ideas that we have long come to see as self-evident: the right of women to receive the same education as men and to be allowed to work in any capacity for which they are fit—doctor, lawyer, senator, and even president. Indeed, by the start of the twenty-first century, those advocates of the politics of progress would be astonished to discover how many of their most cherished ideals have been realized. Some of their earlier pet ideas—such as eugenics and Prohibition—have been dropped along the way, but many of their once-shocking ideas have been become commonplace.

Today's progressives can point with pride to the success of their crusades, but this also presents them with a dilemma. Suppose the ghosts of the great nineteenth-century progressives were to rise up and say, "All of our ideals have been fully realized. The future has surpassed our wildest expectations! It seems as if virtually everyone is a progressive now. What more could you possibly ask for? What noble causes are there left to champion?"

In a world in which, by the standards of earlier eras, the average Joe and Jane are progressives, what right do today's progressives have to continue to style themselves as such? If everyone in your society shares the same progressive views, how can you pride yourself as being more progressive? Why not drop the label? If we have made all the progress possible for us to make, then surely any reasonable person has no cause to clamor and agitate for even more progress, but should defend and maintain the degree of progress that has been achieved with such pain and effort. Of course, this is what happens to many of us who, after having started out as flaming radical progressives, become far more tame as we grow older—it's such a well-known phenomenon that there are many adages about it. But for those of us who have watched the American scene for the past sixty years or so, there is a different and far more substantial reason for feeling a sense of mission accomplished. Progress has been made, as every boomer can attest from his own experience.

Yet none of this seems to satisfy today's progressives. If they were content to simply argue that there was still much to be done to improve the lives of the poor, or help those who need better medical treatment, conservatives might well disagree with them on the best way to achieve these worthwhile ends, but they would be speaking the same language in their debate. But what is most startling about the contemporary progressive is his denial of the very progress that his predecessors were able to bring about during the last six decades, in the United States and many other parts of the globe.

Today, according to the Woke progressive, the once popular doctrine of white supremacy is not an abandoned relic of a superseded past but a clear and present danger to the America of 2024. Fascism is not a long-discredited political movement from an Italy that existed a century ago, it is the core ideological belief of their neighbors who happen to vote Republican. Racism is not the rancid abuse of blacks through violence and intimidation, accompanied by a denial of their most basic human rights, as it was in the segregated South prior to the Civil Rights Act of 1964. It is not the burning of crosses by hooded Klansmen, or lynching of blacks by angry, drunken mobs. No, today there are racist highways, as the secretary of transportation tells us, and even the American love of swimming was born out of racism, according to Gisele Barreto Fetterman. Hardly a day passes now without a progressive politician, pundit, or celebrity finding racism lurking in some hitherto unsuspected corners of our everyday existence, and denouncing it with the righteous fury of a Savonarola. Forgetting their own history of suffering from the blind bigotry of others, litigious gay men and women seek out Christian bakeries to harass with legal suits, simply because their owners' deeply held convictions forbid them from designing wedding cakes for gay marriages. Just how burning a grievance is it that, in a world full of bakeries happy to make wedding cakes for gay marriages, there remain a handful that cannot in good conscience comply?

This is where Ricardo's law of diminishing returns comes into play. The farmer invests in his most fertile fields first. The progressives in the past did the same, choosing to invest their energy in the most glaring grievances of their time: the abolition of slavery, the rights of women, fair treatment for workers, social welfare for the needy, the rights of gays to live in dignity. As these social ills were remedied, it has become more difficult to find genuinely worthy causes. Thus, the law of diminishing returns has forced today's progressives to plough some very barren fields.

Is passing laws to force bakers to make gay wedding cakes against their will really equivalent to the noble causes championed by earlier progressives? Back in the 1950s and early '60s, to be considered a wild-eyed radical, it was enough merely to believe that gay men should not be imprisoned, castrated, or even executed, for that matter. Today, on the other hand, when your old fuddy-duddy Uncle George has a gay favorite bowling partner, it is far more challenging to find a flag to wave that others haven't waved already. The whole point in adopting the identity of an advanced thinker is that everyone else should be a good distance behind you. So what do you do when you suddenly feel the breath of your Aunt Martha on your neck, assuring you that her son has finally found the man of his dreams, and how excited she is about their upcoming nuptials? Obviously, you must run a lot faster.

It is the very success of the progressive agenda over the last century and a half that the woke must ignore if they are to preserve their flattering self-image. This is why they have been reduced to elevating transgender rights as the new litmus test of progressivism. Few would argue that trans people have as much right to live their lives as everyone else, but do their rights automatically trump the rights of everyone else? Did the fight for women's rights mean nothing, so that girls today should be forced to take showers with anatomically intact males or to compete with them in sports, just because these men identify as females?

There is another possible response to the law of diminishing returns faced by today's progressives. Their predecessors took up specific causes, applying intellect and energy to devise specific laws addressing their chosen issue. Indeed, it was precisely their careful attention to detail that ultimately secured their many victories. But the so-called "causes" of today's woke are glittering abstractions, like social justice and racial equity. They are so slippery that it is impossible to get ahold of them. What do they really mean? How would we even know whether we were getting closer to these vague and amorphous goals? Yet it is precisely this quality of indeterminate vagueness that makes them so appealing to the woke. They get a thrill out of championing these pseudo causes, which give them a self-congratulatory high, like a dose of amphetamines. They provide the woke with the illusion of being on the right side of history, when in fact they are the same old utopian dreams of the nineteenth century, recycled for contemporary consumption, dressed up to look all new.

But are we perhaps taking the woke movement too seriously? It is entirely possible that in the long run, or even short run, the woke will wake up to their folly and return to the fold of the sane. In short, is it all just another fad?

There are few questions in sociology more vexing than how and why certain fashions take hold and then, having run their course, become obsolete, even comical, to later generations—like the bell-bottom paisley pants that seemed so cool in the '60s. Or how, for that matter, they all at once become cool again. But at bottom, this pursuit of "coolness," or knowing what is "hip," drives the engine of fashion, though often the only way of knowing for sure that you are cool and hip is by eschewing and avoiding what is not; flee the banal, the humdrum, the old-fashioned, and you will have made a good start. Then observe what the certifiably cool are doing: What are Hollywood stars wearing as evening dress? What does *Architectural Digest* suggest for designing your bedroom and bath? Fortunately, for those who like to stay up-to-date in their opinions and ideas, there are celebrity intellectuals to help us out by saying the kind of trendy things that would never have occurred to us. For ideas and opinions, like clothes and décor, must be changed often if you are not to find yourself stuck in the rut of the old-fashioned and out-of-date.

Snobbery is endemic to human nature, perhaps even unavoidable. It was our original sin, after all; Eve was led into sin when the serpent whispered in her ear, "Ye shall be as gods." That was certainly moving up in the world, and subsequent generations have followed the course she set.

There can be snobbery in politics as well as in matters of taste. Though no sociologist could ever devise a scientific methodology to determine the question, it would be interesting to know how many have been drawn to the woke movement out of sheer snobbery. To be woke permitted them to feel superior to ordinary working-class Americans, on whom they heap their undisguised contempt, while indulging in paranoid fantasies about the sinister designs of White Christian Nationalists (as over half the population of the United States is invariably referred to by woke pundits on MSNBC). Snobbery can be an end in itself, and what it requires is not an ideology but an excuse. And who better to feel superior to than those who have the bad taste to be on the wrong side of history?

Yet integral to the new woke socialism is a feature that radically distinguishes it from any previous form of socialism. Previous versions were optimistic, some wildly and fantastically so. Just recall Charles Fourier's oceans of lemonade. Today, in brutal contrast, the woke socialists predict a vanishing ocean, devastating hurricanes of hitherto unknown fury, and wildfires raging across the landscape, with millions displaced and trying to flee increasing heat waves that have come with global warming. These woke socialists insist vehemently that something must be done now to stop what is to come later. What must be done now, needless to say, requires a vast project of social engineering—far more radical and extensive than any of the Soviet Union's Five-Year Plans.

To keep our kids from dying from climate change, the traditional sources of energy must be abandoned—chiefly fossil fuels, including oil and coal—the very agents by which industrial and technological progress has been achieved in the last three centuries. Nuclear energy, that ambiguous gift of the twentieth century, could provide a suitable alternative. For many decades now, France has made it the source of over 70 percent of its energy needs without a single adverse incident, and they could in theory draw all their energy from nuclear power. Yet this solution is rejected out of hand; it is not a "clean" source, it is said. But if the fate of mankind were really at stake, should the relatively minor risks of nuclear energy count against "saving the planet"?

The unintended consequences of mandating only "green" energy sources like windmills and solar panels are not hard to foresee. They inevitably lead to a reduction in global energy use, bringing along with it a reduction in the quality of the lives of ordinary people, even more so in less-developed nations. Since ordinary people are not apt to agree to their lifestyles being sacrificed to the noble cause of going green, it is obvious that decisions about such matters cannot be left in their hands. Hence the need to give maximal power to the enlightened elite, who—by means of alarmist propaganda and new schemes of social engineering—may save us yet. Trust the jetsetters to Davos. Let them work it out. Though we may well wonder if the adverse consequences of these schemes are really so "unintended" after all. Inflicting the cost of such programs on ordinary people will certainly not affect the lifestyle of those who can afford to fly their jets to conferences where they decide how the Ninety-Nine Percent must live—they will surely be spared.

For many, this might seem a rather strange idea of progress, to have of a tiny minority of the world's population establishing programs to reduce the quality of life for everyone but themselves. But there is another threat that the politics of apocalypse pose to free and open societies. When told we must act immediately or else mankind faces imminent extinction, what possible response can there be except to abandon normal debate and discussion, sober weighing of evidence, or searching for a reasonable compromise—all of which has been the hallmark, the indispensable precondition of liberal democracies? Indeed, no one is more aware of this fact than those whose are most alarmed by their apocalyptic visions, and who therefore feel morally justified in silencing dissent, taking decisions out of the hands of those who do not share their urgency, circumventing the tedious and drawn-out process by which democracies decide what actions need to be taken.

Democracies have always had an Achilles' heel. Their slow and deliberate methods, which function reasonably well under normal circumstances, are not suitable in the face of a grave emergency. Few people have been more dedicated to preserving their republican form of government than the ancient Romans, but they recognized that serious threats—those now dubbed existential—required putting dictatorial power in the hands of a single individual. This office, however, came with a time limit. Once the crisis was over, normal republican governance returned. Later republics would not be so lucky. Although the dictators of the twentieth century are often seen as power-mad individuals who somehow "seized" power, their opportunity came as the result of crises and emergencies that normal parliamentary government was simply unable to handle. They were handed power, often with a sigh of relief from a public that could not see any other way out of their dire situation. But if popular governments of the past were unable to handle their local and specific emergencies, how can modern democracies deal with the greatest threat ever faced by humanity (according to President Joe Biden)?

With such alarming prospects, it has become virtually forbidden to ask the perfectly sensible question: What if the confident predictions of impending apocalypse are simply wrong, or even exaggerated? What if the climate crisis or the further development of artificial intelligence constitute genuine threats, but ones which could nevertheless be handled by the normal process traditional to democratic systems? Once enough power has been invested in an enlightened elite to deal with such existential threats, will this elite relinquish its grasp on power, once the challenge has been met—or, even more worrisome, if the challenge in fact turns out to be less apocalyptic than anticipated?

If the myth of "the right side of history" is always dangerous to open, free, and democratic societies, the politics of apocalypse introduces an unparalleled threat. If those on the right side of history are firmly, even fanatically, convinced that they are on a mission to save life on this planet from extinction, or even to avert the collapse of civilization, then those on the wrong side of history are not merely political opponents but an existential threat who must be silenced or eliminated "by any means necessary." Normal politics cannot hope to survive when the Forces of Light are arrayed against the Forces of Darkness. Manichean politics is an oxymoron: good cannot compromise with evil, and angels cannot strike bargains with the devil.

As noted earlier, this binary approach to politics is reflected in the simplistic reading of the history offered by woke historians. Unable to see beyond their own immediate horizons, they cannot find anything of value in mankind's past, smugly convinced that they singularly have seen the light. The simplistic "good guy versus bad guy" narrative of the past makes it impossible for them to admire any historical figures who have failed the woke litmus test of the moment. And who would not fail by those standards?

But refusing to acknowledge the heroes of the past, warts and all, is dangerous blindness. While we do not live in Vico's Age of Heroes, it is still possible for us to admire the heroic ideal. *The Iliad* continues to cast its magical spell because there is something that will always be deeply moving in Achilles's choice of a short but glorious life over a long but obscure one. The capacity to respect and even admire what heroic men and women have done in other epochs, and for reasons that are not our own, is not historical relativism but an expression of our humanity. The famous quote from the Roman comic dramatist Terence, which Montaigne so admired, still holds true for us when we survey the past: "I am a man, I count nothing human as foreign to me" (*Homo sum, humani nihil a me alienum puto*).

Appreciating the virtues and ethical principles upon which our ancestors acted, even when we think they acted wrongly, does not require us to abandon our own set of values, but is an indispensable precondition of testing and examining them, of making certain that the values we hold are not merely those we have blindly taken on faith, or the fad of the moment. It is through appraising and weighing the truths that were sacred to those of the past that we can come to feel any confidence that our own are not merely trendy truths du jour, picked at random from the groupthink we are surrounded by. It is only through the study of what men did and thought, or hoped and feared in the past that we can learn to know our own minds.

The current woke wave, with its insistence that it alone has found the truth—hitherto unknown and unsuspected by our ancestors—requires cancelling not just those guilty of thought crimes today but yesterday's guilty as well. The woke have begun with the monuments of the past— the statues of heroes—but they may well end by following the example of Mercier's Parisians of 2440: burning all those outdated books from the past that do not reflect their own current woke ideals (including those published only a month before, given the rapidly changing standard of being "woke enough"). The totalitarian impulse to control the future has always demanded the abolition of the past.

This is because the past challenges us. It is full of ethical ambiguity, of people with conflicting duties, honorable men who served bad causes, heroes who fought for the wrong side, noble illusions that ended in disaster, selfish men who fulfilled a higher purpose than they had ever intended. It is understandable that this is a disturbing truth to those who like to keep things simple: the sheep clearly divided from the goats, and the "good things" from the "bad things." The opponents of postmodernism, who insist that we can escape the ambiguity of history because they have discovered universal values or objective truth by which both past and present can be judged, appear to forget that, as Vico argued, the very idea of universal values and objective truth only emerges in his third age, when men turn to reflection. In the two earlier ages, no one suspected the existence of such an idea. In the fourth age, this reflection turns barbarous, at which point the idea that there are universal values or objective truth undergoes a thorough deconstruction, such as has occurred in our own day with postmodernism. But in any actual historical struggle, the claim of one party to possess universal values and objective truth has never yet won a single battle. The other side has its own values and truth as well, and the contest is to determine not which side is right but which side ends up on top. But then, history has never been made by disinterested observers seeking to establish universal verities with which all instinctively agree—for there are none—but by passionate advocates of one side or another.

CONCLUSION

As we move toward the end of the first quarter of the twenty-first century, one thing is certain: optimism is no longer the default mode of our forecasts about the future. Yet those offering their visions of an imminent apocalypse are no less certain that they are on the right side of history than their progressive predecessors, for whom utopia lay right around the corner. As we have seen in this book, the unbridled optimism of these utopians ultimately ended in either folly or disaster, but this was not due to their optimism as such, but to their absolute certainty that the future would unfold exactly in accordance with their plans. The pessimism that we found in classical antiquity might serve as a cautionary warning against excessive self-confidence, but a revival of such blanket pessimism would be fatal for the modern world. What we need instead is a return to the cautious optimism that has served us so well, an optimism tempered by the unavoidable hazards that arise from the law of unintended consequences, an optimism that is not so damn cocksure of itself.

Cautious optimism, when it must deal with challenges such as climate change or the advent of AI, will not be inclined to drastic experiments in social engineering, irremediably prone to unpredictable and often undesirable outcomes, but to a steady incremental approach. It will take each problem as it arises and look at the solutions that are already available. The refusal of woke climate alarmists even to consider nuclear energy as a realistic option to reduce the use of fossil fuels is a striking example of the triumph of utopian thinking over practical good sense.

In the end, it is only by application of practical good sense that we can hope to deal successfully with any of the challenges we currently face. Those who imagine that such challenges as climate change or AI can be met by vast global programs in which all nations agree to act as one—in the general interest of mankind and not for their own narrow self-interests—are displaying the same naïveté about human nature as the Abbé de Saint-Pierre exhibited in his schemes for a world government. Such schemes have always found favor in the eyes of progressives, who are convinced that only a single world government can solve the multitude of problems facing the human race. But today we are no closer to that goal than in the days of Saint-Pierre. It is as much of a utopian daydream as Fruitlands or Brook Farm.

The spirit of cautious optimism, when faced with a challenge, will not turn to despair but will recall how many times in the past equally formidable challenges were met with a considerable measure of success. When President Biden gravely tells the world that the climate crisis is the greatest existential threat mankind has ever faced, has he completely forgotten that not so long ago the specter of nuclear holocaust haunted the dreams of people across the world? Many at the time, including distinguished philosophers and scientists, were certain that such a fate was unavoidable, and yet it has been avoided. To abandon all hope is not the way of cautious optimism, which prefers tinker and experiment and grope toward a practical resolution that will at least have the advantage of avoiding the worst.

The popularity of doomsday scenarios in our time leads us to a troubling question. Is the West now experiencing an end to optimism, a renunciation of all those noble prospects and glorious ventures that the advanced thinkers of the past, including many of America's founding fathers, devoutly put their faith in? And if so, what does that bode for the West? Can a civilization long endure that sees no glimmer of hope as it scans the horizon?

How civilizations die is a question that has long been pondered by historians and philosophers. It would be impossible to survey all the various theories put to forth just to explain the fall of the Roman empire. In 1984, the German historian Alexander Demandt counted 210 different theories, and no doubt more have been added since then. But when Edward Gibbon took up this question in the eighteenth century, he blamed the decline and fall of Rome on two primary factors: the triumph of barbarism and religion, by which he meant Christianity. The German barbarians were too wild and free, having no interest in the strict discipline that had made Rome great, while Christianity subverted the tough Roman ethos by introducing an entirely new set of ethical ideals which turned the old ethos on its head. The founder of Christianity championed the lowly and meek while condemning the high and mighty. He preached the doctrine of passive resistance, though Rome had not become a great empire by turning the other cheek. Christianity taught that pity and compassion were the noblest qualities to which men could aspire, and to love your neighbor, whether a slave or an outcast leper. Most shocking of all, he told his followers that they must love their enemy; how far could Rome have advanced as an empire by practicing such an unworldly policy? Conquer your enemies before they conquer you—that had been the traditional Roman approach prior to the coming of Christianity.

Yet long before either barbarians or Christians appeared on the scene, there were many intelligent Romans, like the historian Livy, who already saw the symptoms of decline all around him. His own great history of Rome was written between 27 and 9 BC, during the Age of Augustus, the very point in time that Gibbon had taken for his starting point in his own work. Livy pins the blame for this sad state of affairs on the vast influx of wealth that had come with Rome's triumphal conquest of the Mediterranean world in the previous centuries. Such new riches had led to excessive luxury and effeminacy of manner—the loss of the hard, virile ethos that Livy had illustrated with his stories of the exemplary conduct of earlier Romans.

Yet Cato the Elder, who died in 149 BC, over a century before Livy began his work, was no less concerned with the loss of the manly virtues of early Rome, though, in addition to the bane of too much wealth and luxury, he foresaw the perils attendant on the budding taste for Greek philosophy among the youth of his day. Cato's attitude toward Greek philosophy is well-illustrated by an anecdote Plutarch relates of him. In 155 BC, when Cato was advanced in years, the Athenians sent a delegation to Rome. Its mission was to try to persuade the Romans to remit a fine of five hundred talents that had been imposed on their city. But there was something quite remarkable about Athens's selection of its delegates. Rather than sending professional diplomats to plead their case, they sent professional philosophers—three of them, the most prominent being Carneades, whom we briefly met in an earlier chapter, and who was celebrated in his native land as the leading skeptic philosopher of his day.

Cato was present for Carneades's debut performance as Athens's ambassador. In his speech, the philosopher took up the subject of the nature of justice, which had long been one of the more critical questions in Greek ethical theory. Carneades proceeded to praise the Romans for their own high tradition of practicing justice in their affairs with other powers. This approach was astute; the Romans took great pride in being just. No doubt this was a form of self-congratulation, yet there was some solid evidence to back up their claim. By flattering the Romans as just men, Carneades was hoping to win them over to his side, to wit: "Our case is just. You are just men. Therefore, you must render us justice." But this shrewd buttering-up of his listeners was only Carneades's first move. The following night, he gave another lecture, only this time he offered a devastating refutation of all the points he had made the night before. Applying to the idea of justice the dialectical skills of the professional skeptic, he argued that justice, like truth, was unknowable. At best, what was called justice was simply an arbitrary convention that human beings had worked out among themselves in order to achieve a reasonable degree of peace and stability in a society.

The Romans were stunned, but many of them, especially the young, were also intrigued and delighted. No one had ever told young Romans to question what their culture took for granted as justice or truth. Alarmed by this response, Cato gave orders to have the philosopher return by fast boat to Athens. It was self-evident to him that when a society begins to grow skeptical of the traditional values it has handed down through centuries, it becomes like a man who undermines the foundation of his own house and then is surprised when it falls on top of him. Rome's only hope of staying great was by preserving those hard virtues that had made Rome great.

In Vico's philosophy of history, the universal skepticism of Carneades was symptomatic of the fourth and final stage of any civilization, the barbarism of reflection—the stage in which the Greece of Cato's day had already entered. Such sweeping skepticism, if it gained a hold in popular thought, would inevitably overmine the self-confidence of any civilization, rendering it not only doubtful about its traditional values, but profoundly uncertain of its future. Cato immediately saw the danger that the Greek penchant for radical skepticism posed both to the tradition and to the mission of Rome.

Cato's views about Rome and Greece might be distilled into an aphorism: A society begins to decline when it no longer believes in itself and in its future, and it will inevitably yield to those who believe their future is before them—as the philosophically perplexed Greeks were eventually subjugated by Romans, with their uncritical veneration of their tough traditional ethos. A society that sees no hope in its future will be hard put to justify its continuing existence.

Today, however, many Americans not only see nothing to hope for in our future but nothing to admire in our past. For many progressives, it has become an article of faith that Europeans should never have set foot in the New World, which is another way of saying that our own culture and society should never had come into being. What society has ever wished that it had never been born? None—this again is something new under the sun. A people who regret that they ever had a past cannot hope to have much of a future. Perhaps the advocates of voluntary human extinction do not represent a fringe but the sad shape of things to come—at least in America.

There are various ways in which a society can lose confidence in its own future. Total defeat through subjugation is certainly one, although it is still possible to retain hope even in the face of apparent adversity, as the exiled Hebrews amply proved after the destruction of their city and temple by the Babylonians. But such hope is only possible for those who are convinced that, no matter what adversity they presently face, the future will vindicate them. Churchill expressed this hope of the desperate when he told Soviet Ambassador Ivan Maisky the well-known story about the two rats who found themselves in a bucket of cream with no way out. One rat was intelligent enough to see that his fate was hopeless, and drowned. The foolish rat simply kept on swimming for his life, and in the morning found himself alive and well, though exhausted, on top of a pail of butter.

Yet, as we have seen, it is all too possible to believe in a future that fails to come to pass. Even worse are those examples from history in which a fanatical conviction that "tomorrow belongs to us" has led true believers to assume that they are on the right side of history, when in fact they are on a direct path to history's trash bin. This was the fate of Italian fascism, German National Socialism, and Soviet Communism. Each shared the certainty that they were working to create a New Man—the Man of the Future. Mussolini wanted to instill in his fellow Italians a futuristic version of the antique Roman martial spirit, but one equipped with the most up-to-date military technology, embracing the speed and efficiency that was the hallmark of the modern world. Hitler and the National Socialists aimed at regenerating a supposed Aryan master race. The New Man, as conceived by the Nazis, would be a racially purified exemplar of Nietzsche's Übermensch—the Superman, liberated at last from the sickly sentimentalism of the slave morality that Christianity had taught. He would be beyond good and evil, inured to the contemptible softness that wallowed in compassion and pity. He would recognize the fallacy behind the liberal illusion that progress consists of promoting democracy, with its absurd assumption that all men were equal and should be given equal rights. True progress, on the contrary, required the total repudiation of liberalism in all its manifestations, and could only come about when the National Socialists' New Man took his rightful place as master of the world.

The New Man promised by the Soviet Union was a different creature altogether. Selfless and utterly devoted to the welfare of his fellow toilers, the Soviet New Man was above wanting to be paid for the work he did. He would do it joyfully and cheerfully, assured in his noble heart that his efforts were leading to the dawn of a world transfigured: the Workers' Paradise. The gratitude of his comrades was enough to inspire truly prodigious feats of labor. For example, Aleksey Stakhanov was celebrated both at home and abroad as representing the Soviet idea of the New Man, a true Hero of Labor. Let all follow his shining example, and Karl Marx's prophecies of the end of history would surely follow.

The idea of the New Man can be traced back to those optimists in the Age of Enlightenment who held the conviction that human nature was almost infinitely malleable. It could be shaped and formed in accordance with a blueprint drawn up by the enlightened elite—the elect of history— provided they were given control over the education and rearing of children, lest they be contaminated and corrupted by the insidious influence of their own benighted parents and family.

How much control was enough? Earlier we noted the naïve faith these early enlightened optimists placed in law and institutions. They believed that if they were permitted to draw up just the right laws and to create just the right institutions, the people subject to them would instantly abandon their erring ways, and be transformed into the rational and noble creature that man was originally meant to be, but which the wicked laws and institutions of the past had denied them.

The folly of the French Revolution was that it took this faith quite literally, and proceeded in the first great effort to create the New Man out of freshly made laws and newly minted institutions, all of which were designed in accordance with the indisputable principle of reason. Unfortunately, the New Men in charge of bringing enlightenment to the masses quickly discovered that the Goddess of Reason is a tease. She convinces one man that he holds her in his arms, while she deceives another into believing he is her beloved, then watches with a complacent smile as her cheated lovers begin to cut each other's heads off—though with greatly improved methods.

The heads that fell from the guillotine were the first victims of the right side of history. The Girondists came first; they did not share the vision of the future that the Jacobins embraced, thereby being convicted by their own words and actions that they were on the wrong side of history. Enemies of the future, they had to be condemned. Brennus, when he seized Rome with the help of his hardy Gallic warriors, coined the phrase "Woe to the vanquished" (*Vae victis*). But still greater woe awaits those unfortunates who are found to be on the wrong side of history by those who are absolutely certain that they are on the right side. The Soviet gulags were designed for such renegades, while China under Mao Zedong sent those who were not shot to be reeducated by the right-siders. Even those convinced that liberal democracy was the wave of the future showed little compunction when they began systemic bombing of civilian populations in the Second World War. The vanquished Germans after the war were subjected to horrendous treatment—not the leaders who deserved it but women and children who surely did not. In general, the more deeply men are convinced that they are on the right side of history, the more merciless they are to those they regard as being on the wrong side. The evidence of this unhappy truth is scattered across the globe in millions of graves, both known and unknown, in which rest people whose only crime was that they stood in the way of other people's futures.

The totalitarian impulse lurks wherever there is the urge to create the New Man and to bid farewell to Old Adam. Because it takes much more than enlightened laws and institutions to create the New Man, the enlightened elite come to recognize that the only way their mission can be accomplished is if they eliminate from society any element that might hinder their objective. This requires maximal control over not just over laws and institutions but over the totality of the society they are remolding: its cultural life, music, literature, popular pastimes, favorite sports, youth organizations, religion. Nothing can claim exemption that might impede the task of creating the New Man. Even an insignificant instance of dissent must not be permitted but harshly punished.

None of the totalitarian states of the twentieth century—fascist Italy, Nazi Germany, or the USSR—ever came close to achieving the ideal of total control, but they certainly tried. Even in Orwell's novel, *1984*, which depicts the ne plus ultra of totalitarian states, the bulk of society, the proles who made up roughly 90 percent of the population, did not have Big Brother watching over their shoulders. They were left free to guzzle beer and watch football. With the stunning advances in media technology, however, it now becomes possible to influence virtually the entire society, to manufacture public opinion wholesale. The danger inherent in such power should be self-evident, as it certainly would be if it were in the hands of conservatives. Such power should not be in any hands, which becomes glaringly evident when it falls into the wrong hands—which is where it is today.

The power to manufacture public opinion is once again in the hands of an elite that is convinced it is on the right side of history, and intent on getting everyone else on its side, convinced that it has a mission to spread the gospel of woke to the masses. Cancel culture is a symptom of the totalitarian impulse to eradicate even the slightest dissent from the accepted party line du jour. Boomers like myself, who had backed all the progressive causes of our youth, experience an ideological future shock daily, when confronted with our own thought crimes as revealed by the latest woke trend. Who knew that it would become a crime to have even once entertained the idea that males with their genitals intact should not be allow to shower with young girls? Who knew that *ze*, *zie*, *vers*, and *zieself* were pronouns, and that you could get in serious hot water if you didn't know the right one to use when addressing someone? Who knew that it was every elementary schoolchild's God-given right to have teachers explain to them that they could switch genders or have none at all, anytime they want?

Okay, boomer.

True, but old people who are reasonably observant have an advantage that the young do not. We have all been severely disappointed by our hopes for the future. We have seen our imaginary futures fail, including ones that we sincerely believed in. The first time I saw my name in print was in a letter to the editor of the *Atlanta Constitution*, written when I was a lad of fourteen—a rousing defense of democratic socialism. Only after several decades did I bid farewell to my adolescent dream of a more just and equitable world though social engineering, and even then it was only with considerable reluctance. Like a child who wants to keep on believing in Santa Claus, but whose doubts have begun to nag him, I wanted it to be true, yet I could no longer reconcile it with those brutal things called facts. Yet looking back at that fourteen-year-old boy, though I now blush at his naïveté, I still find something to admire in him.

To support democratic socialism in 2024 is to join the crowd. It has become *the* fashionable opinion to have among today's college kids. But back in 1963, in the Deep South where I lived, democratic socialism was hardly a fad. I knew no one else who shared my opinion. I had other heterodox ideas as well, especially about civil rights, and was not shy about expressing them openly. My mother often hinted to me that she would not like to see a cross burning in our front yard some night and could I please be a bit more reticent about my political views. Perhaps I was foolhardy, but I stuck to my guns. Only a year before I had brought down upon my head the wrath of the Baptist Church that I attended by defending Darwin's theory of evolution. There, too, I had stood alone. I was getting used to it.

Though I have changed many of my ideas since that time long ago, I still cannot help recognizing that it took moral courage to stand alone, especially at that young age, when it is so much easier to join the crowd. Today, when I look around at our contemporary political landscape, it is hard to find even a trace of moral courage among those adults in positions of power and authority. University presidents yield to mob pressure on their campuses. Politicians jump on the woke bandwagon simply to get out of its way. They recite like parrots the woke creed of the hour. Everyone seems terrified even to entertain unpopular positions, let alone to take a public stand on them.

When I look at protesting college students, I see only a crowd—and moral courage has never been at home in a crowd. Whether they are vociferously intimidating speakers whose ideas offend them, such as Ben Shapiro or Heather Mac Donald; or attacking J. K. Rowling, whose books they grew up reading but whose commonsense insistence on the basic facts of biology they find abhorrent; or chanting in unison for the destruction of Israel, I see only the manifestations of groupthink, that inveterate enemy of moral courage. Perhaps it is just human nature to go along with the crowd, but wisdom has never been found in one.

Back in the fifties, when I grew up, intellectuals endlessly upbraided ordinary Americans for their passion for conformism, their fear of disagreeing with the majority. Today, however, the bastions of conformism have become our universities, even our greatest ones, and it is the intellectuals who are the first to decry and vilify anyone who dares to question the prevailing political orthodoxy of the day. Part of this may be explained by the gradual transformation of public education into a system of political indoctrination, in which invincibly sincere teachers are molding the minds of the young to conform with their own agendas. Part may be explained by the prevalence of social media, where so-called influencers shape to their will the impressionable minds of those eager to go along with the fashions and fads of the moment. Yet perhaps the most important factor is that courage itself is no longer seen as a virtue worth cultivating. It smacks too much of that trendy bugbear known as "toxic masculinity."

Mine was a generation inspired by John F. Kennedy's book *Profiles in Courage*. The courage in question was not physical courage, such as fighting off a bear or climbing Mount Everest. It was moral courage. The book told the stories of those Americans who, stirred deeply by their own conscience, took widely unpopular stands on a variety of issues. Their stories are noble and uplifting, and it is difficult not to regard them as heroes, even in those cases when we ourselves might disagree utterly with the stand they took. But we live in an age from which the hero—both the physical hero and the moral hero—has been banished from history. The figures that previously inspired the young by their shining examples of courage in the face of immense odds have all been debunked. One by one, their statues are being removed or defaced. Books dwell not on their virtues but on their all too human defects. Indeed, any figure of the past who fails to check all the woke boxes of virtue-signaling is doomed to be regarded as a contemptible reactionary, including those who in their own time were considered the vanguard of progress, such as George Washington and Thomas Jefferson.

When discussing the subject of this book with friends, I have been asked: How can we keep our own kids from becoming the woke sheep that are running amok today? How can we inoculate them so that they are immune to the ideological pathogens in the very air they breathe? How, in short, can we provide them with the moral courage necessary to resist the call of the crowd? The answer is to give them something to believe in as a child, which is only possible if you believe in something yourself. Let me try to explain by offering another personal story from the '60s.

My mother had a cousin whose husband was a graduate of Princeton. They both had self-consciously advanced opinions and ideas. The cousin told my mom that they had decided not to impose their own ideas and values on their two children. They would let their kids think for themselves and discover what religion or philosophy suited them best. They would simply make sure to keep their children's bodies snug, warm, and healthy, but as to their minds, the kids were on their own. I was appalled. I had never heard a crazier idea. Children needed something to believe in, as I had been taught to believe—something serious, solid, and fixed. To raise them without this moral foundation would be like exposing your children to nature by dropping them in the middle of a vast jungle and expecting them to find their way out by themselves.

Later, I would come to realize how much this value-free style of parenting had become the vogue among the college-educated, most of whom had learned to be ashamed of their parents. After all, the first lesson instilled in the college students of my day was that their own moms and dads were—horror of horrors!—*ethnocentric*. Their benighted parents believed that their own traditional customs, values, mores, and habits of the heart were right. They were even insistent on imparting their same ethnocentric ways to their offspring. Thus arose the first generation of human beings who were ashamed to raise their children with their own beliefs and values. The alternative to this was precisely the practice to which my mom's cousin and her husband subscribed: letting your kids make up their own minds about things. Don't force them to believe in anything. Let them think for themselves.

Today on Facebook, there are regularly posted memes that children should to be taught to think for themselves, as if that settles the matter. But no one can be *taught* to think for themselves. It is an oxymoron. Those would-be enlighteners, such as Noam Chomsky, who maintain that they can teach others this trick, are deceiving both themselves and those gullible enough to take them at their word. In practice, this teaching others to think for themselves inevitably turns out to mean: don't think like your folks—think like me! Like my mother's cousin, the educated parents of today have often been educated out of their own convictions and have none left to guide their own children. Because children have a sixth sense for sham, they can sense that their parents do not feel qualified to teach them values, having so few themselves. This leaves a void in the soul of the children, though it is one that will be quickly filled by those charlatans and influencers who have no doubts about *their* own convictions. This accounts for why so many children raised in a value-free atmosphere at home are so susceptible to cultish fads that promise them the moral certitude denied them by their parents.

In the final analysis, it does not matter so much what convictions the parents have, so long they hold them deeply and convey this faith in their own beliefs to their children, without hesitation or reservation. My own parents never had any doubt about what they believed and thought important, and this was emphatically relayed to me as a kid. I knew where they stood, unambiguously and without a hint of equivocation. The idea of teaching me to think for myself certainly never crossed their minds. And yet, by the age of fourteen, I had taken the first baby steps in the lifelong project of learning to think for myself. This was not despite my upbringing but because of it. I had been given a set of very firm ideas by my parents, and at some point, I began to wonder about them. Were they all true? Were some of the ideas inconsistent with others?

Such doubts can arise only *after* a child has been given something to believe in first. Teaching a child to question everything, to doubt all he is told, as some would have us do, ensures that child will never make it to the multiplication tables, let alone do any serious thinking about more important questions. So unnatural is a childhood raised in unresolved doubt that it is little wonder that the products of such a school of skepticism will often rush into the arms of the first peddler of absolute certitude, against which he will have no natural immunity, never having ever known anyone before who believed in much of anything.

Today, these peddlers of absolute certitude claim to be on the right side of history, as if that alone were enough to guarantee the validity of their cause. In this book, I have tried to show both the fallacy and danger inherent in such sweeping claims. The woke movement, by attempting to refashion human nature according to its ideals, to create a New Man, is a new variation on an old theme. The New Man promised by socialists of all persuasions never appeared, his new dawn never came. Nor did it come for Nordic man, the Übermensch announced by Nietzsche, who turned out to be not more than human but far less. We are stuck with Old Adam, the most stubborn fact of all. We must do with him the best we can.

With enough magical thinking, even the most stubborn facts can be ignored, but only for so long—usually the time it takes for those stubborn facts to take their revenge by tossing into your face a future that you never had imagined. It is the continual power of the future to shock that has doomed all the various schemes predicated on the idea of historical determinism, the philosophy of history that holds that the present is nothing more than the inevitable outcome of the past. It asserts that if we could know all the relevant historical information from the past, we could predict not only the present but the future as well. From the determinist's point of view, our common idea of the future turns out to be an illusion.

Our assumption that by our actions we can change the future is solely the result of our imperfect knowledge of the past.

All those ideologies that convinced their followers that they were on the right side of history are variations on the theme of historical determinism. You knew you were on the right side of history because your ideology of choice told you just where history was going, and even how it was to end. Yet none of these ideologies got the future right; indeed, virtually all of them got it totally and horrendously wrong.

The power of history to surprise should also be taken into account by those on the Left who warn of a coming fascist takeover in the United States, as well as those on the Right who warn that the nation is about to be delivered into the hands of communists. Both may well be right to warn of a coming threat to our survival as a democracy—or even the survival of the modern West—but whatever this threat turns out to be, it will not be a replay of the past. It will be a future of our own making, due to our own mistakes and errors. As the English historian A. J. P. Taylor remarked in his biography of Otto von Bismarck, "Great disasters are caused by trying to learn from history and to correct past mistakes. It is probably better to think about the present, not about the past, or the future."

History itself is the best refutation of historical determinism and the dangerous false sense of confidence that it provides. Throughout this book, we have seen how the present moment, at any given point in history, is the result not only of the past but also of the futures imagined at the time. There are moments when our imagined future is by far the most powerful motivator of our actions in the present, like the Christian martyrs who, rather than renounce their faith in the next world, voluntarily accepted an agonizing death in this one, or the devout Communist who gladly sacrificed his own life in order to hasten the advent of the Workers' Paradise. All such cases testify to the paradoxical power of the future to shape the present. The future, as something we can change, may be an illusion, but it has been an illusion that people have taken seriously enough to change the world.

In his classic book *The Idea of Progress*, historian J. B. Bury coined the phrase "the illusion of finality" to express the premise that underlies so many of our ideas about the future—namely that history is moving toward some kind of grand finale. This finale could be the Second Coming or the Workers' Paradise, so long as it represented the goal to which history had been moving all along. The desire to see a happy ending to history is a potent persuader, yet it is one that has misled people in the past, their dreams of a glorious future blinding them to the bitter disappointment that history had in store for them.

It should be noted that the Illusion of Finality is a distinctly Western notion. The religions of India hold that just as there was an infinite amount of time behind us, so there is an infinite amount of time ahead of us. When a single *kalpa* might last over a billion years in their reckoning of time, the Illusion of Finality has no place. The very numbers themselves seem more designed to boggle the mind than to enlighten it. Who among puny mortals, with our mere three score years and ten, can even begin to comprehend such unfathomable immensities? But that is the very point of the analogy: to stress the utter insignificance of mortal endeavors by putting them into the perspective of an endless round of death and rebirth. Nothing we do really matters, after all—hence there is no point in recording it. This may explain why ancient India, despite its brilliant accomplishments in every other field of creative endeavor, left behind no history—not even a single reliable date, until Alexander the Great entered the subcontinent in 327 BC—a fact preserved for us by Callisthenes of Olynthus, the professional historian whom he took along to record his deeds.

Perhaps history can only remain important to us as long as we don't have too much of it. A simple thought experiment will make this clear. Imagine that you are living in the year 1,000,000 AD. There is nothing inherently impossible about this prospect, so long as human beings do not figure out a way to annihilate themselves or their planet, (assuming as well that we are not brought low by factors beyond our control, such as the return of another Ice Age or the impact of another asteroid like that one that killed the dinosaurs—this last peril the one that most concerned theoretical physicist Stephen Hawking).

With a million years of human history behind you, what interest could you possibly take in it? Perhaps an antiquarian hobbyist might have an eccentric interest in a certain period of the past—say, the age of Charlemagne—but who could hope to even begin to encompass its immense expanse? And if it could be done, what would be the point of doing it? Today, there are a number of books that take as their subject the history of the world, most of them rather lengthy tomes. But how many volumes would be required to write such a history in 1,000,000 AD—or, for that matter, in 10,000 AD?

Too much future and our mind boggles. Like Macbeth contemplating an endless series of tomorrows, we come to look on our own lives as "signifying nothing" when set against the immeasurable backdrop of eternity. No one will remember that we lived or what we did, either an individuals or societies, a million years from now—but will anyone care a thousand years from now, or a century, or even a decade?

This is why the Illusion of Finality has dominated so much of Western thinking, both religious and secular. The peoples of the West, going back to the first Christians and throughout the Middle Ages, always believed that the end was near, that the Second Coming was just around the corner. The big round year, 1000 AD, was an obvious milestone, though when it passed without incident, 1100 AD seemed like the next obvious choice. The Future Revolution of the nineteenth-century visionaries—perhaps surprisingly, given its embrace of science—did not conceive of the future in terms of millions of years. On the contrary, the glorious future they imagined was waiting right around the corner. The time clock of the universe might continue to run, but history would have a stop.

Yet it is an open question whether the Illusion of Finality is a "good thing" or a "bad thing."

On the one hand, the Illusion of Finality has been constructive because it has provided human beings with a goal that they can work toward. What progress has been made by mankind is indebted to it. On the other hand, the Illusion of Finality has just as frequently beguiled men into thinking that they were marching on the right side of history. It has compelled them to take militant action, in complete confidence that they could do no wrong. This is why boomers like me are naturally inclined to skepticism about those who claim they see the future clearly before them and insist that we must see it too. Our survey of futures past is perhaps the best antidote to those who promise us a utopia, as well as those who see only gloom and doom ahead of us. Unlike books that deal with a future whose outcome remains unknown to us, this book has considered futures that have come and gone, as well as futures that never arrived at all. Sadly, the history of futures past is largely a record of folly, deluded hope, and disappointment. If there is a lesson here for today, it is that any prediction about the future should be met with an awareness of the dangers of false hopes and of false fears, and how often those who have been most certain about the future have proved to be most wrong.

Here we find perhaps the best reason to study the past. History cannot teach us to foresee the future, but it can teach us to be wary of those who claim they can, especially those who claim that their visions come with an ironclad guarantee of infallibility. All too frequently those who are convinced that they possess the keys to the future have repeatedly led their followers, along with a host of innocent bystanders, to disaster. The danger posed by hubris—the constant theme of the Greeks—remains as potent as ever, although those who today are tempted by it possess powers far exceeding those recounted in the cautionary tales of ancient Greece.

www.ingramcontent.com/pod-product-compliance
Ingram Content Group UK Ltd.
Pitfield, Milton Keynes, MK11 3LW, UK
UKHW021907190726
13853UKWH00002B/547